GERMAN SHORTHAIRED POINTERS TODAY

DAVID LAYTON

HOWELL BOOK HOUSE

New York

HOWELL BOOK HOUSE
A Simon & Schuster Macmillan company
1633 Broadway
New York, NY 10019.
MACMILLAN is a registered trademark of Macmillan, Inc.

Library of Congress Cataloging-in-Publication data

Layton, David.
    German shorthaired pointers today/ David Layton.

        p.   cm.
    ISBN 0-87605-181-6
    1. German shorthaired pointers.   I. Title
    SF429.G4L385   1994
    636.7'52 – dc20

93-39078
CIP

10 9 8 7 6 5 4 3
Printed and bound in Singapore

Contents

Acknowledgements

A book of this nature cannot be written without recourse on the part of the author to what has already been researched and written by others; *The German Shorthaired Pointer Today* is no exception.

Unlimited thanks must go to my two expert informants in the United States of America, Marybeth Kirkland and Dianne Roghair, both of whom worked so diligently on my behalf. Their contributions have been invaluable. Thanks to Bonnie Clark, who has supplied me with information and photographs relating to the GSP in Canada. I am also pleased to acknowledge the willing co-operation of The Canadian Kennel Club in providing me with copies of its rules and giving me permission to quote from them.

I am also indebted to the following ladies for help and information so readily given: Ann Sofie Rundberg and Katarina Kjorling, who have been good enough to supply me with information regarding GSP activities in Scandinavia. Wendy Schwalger and Kathy Hughes of New Zealand; Georgina Byrne, Pat Farnan, Olga Gillies, Dianne Norman (Edelhof) and Renee Luckman of Australia.

Some facts and statements have been gleaned from the following books, and I am grateful to their authors and publishers for permission to quote them. Where this has been done, the acknowledgement is in the text.

Scent – The magazine of The German Shorthaired Pointer Association.

Der Deutche Kurzhaar. Georgina Byrne, Austed Publishing Co.

All Purpose Gundog. David Layton, Dalsetter Designs.

Bailey's Gundog Directory. Burlington Publishing Co.

Shorthair – The magazine of The German Shorthaired Pointer Club of America.

Standards, rules and regulations quoted by permission of: The English Kennel Club, The American Kennel Club, The German Shorthaired Pointer Club of America, The Federation Cynologique Internationale, and the Canadian Kennel Club.

Countless persons have provided photographs, for which I am most grateful. Where the photographer is known, this is acknowledged with the illustration.

My wholehearted thanks to Gerry Myers who so faithfully interpreted my ideas and reproduced them in the diagrams.

Last, but most certainly not least, I acknowledge a great debt to my wife, Mic, for her help and support. She unstintingly put up with my long incarceration in the office, and kept me endlessly supplied, not only with cups of coffee and refreshments, but with snippets of information, which were continually on the tip of my tongue, but could not quite be recalled to order.

Mr and Mrs Howard Fisher's Sh.Ch. Midlander Moonstone   *Howard Fisher.*

Chapter One

BREED ORIGINS AND DEVELOPMENT

SPORTING DOGS

Long before any dictionary contained the word 'gundog', other terms for sporting dogs were in common usage. Mostly those descriptive terms were associated with the special aspect of work for which the particular type of dog was used. They would have been known collectively as 'sporting dogs', though several of them were initially developed as hunters for food – a bird or beast to fill the pot. Another use was to carry out necessary husbandry to keep down predators and vermin.

And so, in advance of gundogs came sporting dogs in variety. There were, and still are, of course, hounds, whose job has changed little with the years. Their job was to hunt down animals, each breed type being specialised for a particular animal: Foxhounds, Otterhounds, Beagles for hunting hares, and so on. The hunting pattern was sufficiently exciting for the activity to become a 'sport' and to be enjoyed by hunter and hound alike. Sporting terriers developed in parallel with hounds and as aids to farmers wishing to reduce vermin. They went to ground to deal with the larger animals, and they caught and killed rats almost faster than the farmer could count when the grain was threshed and the rats were disturbed from the harvested crops.

Birds and animals were hunted for food and for sport. The setting of nets on the mud-flats of river estuaries to catch waders and wildfowl provided food, but offered little or no 'sport'. Using falcons and hawks was perhaps less satisfying to the stomach, but the excitement of the sport was intense. Partridges, a particularly good bird to eat, were netted as they crouched on the ground by day and by night, sought out and held by astute Pointers or Setters.

The dogs were often abetted by a hawk, 'waiting on' above, to further discourage the birds from flight while the hunters crept up with their hopefully all-enveloping nets to throw over the covey of birds. There, surely, was the basic fulfillment of hunting for food and for sport. Indeed, it must have been a heart-stopping exercise with the individual abilities of hawk, dog and man combining to produce the final success. The only losers were the partridges, and even they made their contribution, finally, on a dinner plate!

Thus, in Great Britain and to some extent in parts of Europe, these specialist game-finding dogs, the Pointers and Setters, were developed. There was variety of breeds, but all with the same game-finding capabilities. The stage was now set for the advent of explosives, and the sporting gun and cartridge completed the scenario in which these dogs were to play their true lead-role in the sporting arena.

SPECIALIST GUNDOGS

Some breeds were well established in type and have altered very little since those early days. The

Hungarian Vizsla, the Pointer of Hungary, is probably a fair example of this. In fact, the Pointer of England is another. Old prints, depicting the Pointer on the moors, show only small differences from those photographed in the same role today.

The sport of shooting game developed as a major pastime of the British aristocracy and other wealthy land-owners. These sportsmen tended to specialise, and by the late Victorian and early Edwardian era (in which King Edward VII was himself a leader of the fashion), they had developed the shooting of game birds, aided by a variety of specialist gundogs. The Pointer (together with the Setters of England, Ireland, and the Gordon of Scotland) ran and hunted for game, seeking it with nose alone, and staunchly pointing (or setting) to the presence of game. They ran only in open country – on the heather moors of the North for grouse, the only game birds to live on the high ground – or on the great stubble fields of the South of England, the traditional home of the grey partridge. Those breeds were not expected to enter cover, and nor did they. Their job was done when the birds were presented to the guns.

Retrieving of the shot birds was carried out by the specialist breeds of that name – the Retrievers. On the grouse moors and stubbles they followed the Pointers with their handlers, and 'picked-up' the game after them. The Retrievers also came into their own as the art of driven bird shooting increased. Both pheasants and partridges, the former in the protective cover of woodland, and the latter in their more natural open habitat, were reared – sometimes in huge quantities. They were bred, fed, protected and cosseted until the late autumn and winter, and they were then driven to fly over the guns by 'beaters', whose job it was to ensure that as many birds as possible flew over the waiting line of guns.

This was not simple slaughter; the process was not to make simple shots for the guns. Situations were sought, even contrived, in order that the flying birds were fast and high, demanding a highly accomplished performance from those superbly competent shots. They would not deign to take 'easy' birds, wishing to test their prowess only on the most difficult ones. Retrievers, firstly Flat-coated and Curly-coated, but later Labradors and Goldens had their heyday in those years of the 'big bags', and in due course, the Labrador, particularly, rose to great heights of popularity.

Less formality was attached to cover hunting for game birds and ground game (i.e. rabbits and hares). Here, the Spaniel breeds developed variously and came to excel. Working through the heaviest cover, but always close and within game shot of the guns, they flushed the game into the open to be shot, and retrieved it afterwards. In both these styles of shooting, i.e. over Spaniels, and standing to shoot driven birds, the Pointer had no part to play, but each breed was a specialist in its own field, and one breed did not compete with another.

THE ALL-PURPOSE GUNDOG

The scene in Europe was rather different. Perhaps a desire for all-round thoroughness, particularly by the sportsmen of the teutonic states, led to those hunters looking for and breeding, as they saw it, the perfect one-man dog. They wanted a dog to be sensitive enough, and possessed of a good enough nose, to be able to locate, point and hold game while the guns approached to within shot, to present that game to the guns, and to retrieve it competently afterwards. They also called for a dog with a good 'search nose', to follow and locate larger wounded game, such as deer, and to have the courage and capability to deal with wild or feral cats and foxes. Additionally, they insisted on a sound temperament companion-dog to accompany them on their hunting forays and to protect the home and family.

It was no small task the breeders set themselves! They looked for 'a medium-sized dog, noble but sturdy, showing strength and endurance: a versatile hunter and all-purpose gundog with a very

RIGHT: The German Shorthaired Pointer is the ultimate all-purpose gundog: a versatile hunter, with perseverance in searching and showing initiative in game-finding, and retrieving game tenderly to hand.

BELOW: Madge and Cliff Simons' Ch. and Ft.Ch. Geramer's Victress of Swifthouse.

keen nose, perseverance in searching, and showing initiative in game-finding; equally good on land or in water'. That was the animal they sought to produce in their breeding programme, and they were ruthless in the pursuit of their aim. That was their blue-print, and indeed, those words I have quoted are the very ones incorporated in all the Standards of the German Shorthaired Pointer of today. The aims of the early German idealists were realised, refined, possibly adapted a little to suit the individual requirements of the hunters of a particular country; but today we are the proud trustees of a breed which, at its best, lives up to every dream of those early pioneers.

HUNTING, POINTING, RETRIEVING BREEDS

There are several breeds of Utility gundogs (or sporting dogs) capable in the hunt, point and retrieve role. In addition to German Shorthaired Pointers, there are Longhaired and Wirehaired varieties; the Weimaraner, the so-called grey ghost dog of Germany; the Brittany Spaniel (called simply the Brittany in Britain and the United States); the Hungarian Vizsla; the Large Munsterlander (no more nor less than the black and white German Longhaired Pointer); the Drentze Partridge Dog; the Italian Spinone, and several 'brache' dogs of France, Italy and Spain. None of these latter breeds have found their way much beyond the borders of their own countries of origin.

In the English-speaking countries of the world, the German Shorthaired Pointer stands alone at the head of the group, its capability in the field, together with its admirable temperament, surpassing all the others. As we all know, success breeds success. The GSP was the group leader even before it left its country of origin. Sportsmen are notorious for knowing a good thing when they see one. The advent of the GSP in the United States of America preceded their arrival in Britain by twenty years or more, and almost another twenty years were to elapse before the breed arrived in the Antipodes, firstly in New Zealand and then in Australia. A small number have been in South Africa for many years, owned quietly by individual sportsmen but not bred there in quantities.

EARLY DAYS IN GERMANY

The country of origin, Germany, was, surprisingly, not a single integrated nation during the earliest years of the breed's development, though perhaps there was more co-operation on a canine level than history would suggest there was on a political level. The ending of the wars which held the small states apart, resulted in the emergence of a united Germany as a sovereign nation in 1870, and this event heralded the first three decades of the documented development of the 'Kurzhaar'.

National identity, presumably, gave some cohesion to the efforts which had previously been more individually inspired, making possible the inauguration of the Klub Kurzhaar. This very first breed association in the world for The German Shorthaired Pointer was founded in 1891 from the previously formed Brantiger Klub; and today there are some twenty-five regional breed clubs in Germany under the parental umbrella of the parent Deutsch Kurzhaar Verband (Byrne, *Der Deutsch Kurzhaar*). Old photographs (not always reliable) show tremendous variations of type throughout the latter part of the 19th century, but by the early 1900s dogs were being bred which were very similar to look at, and which behaved in the accepted way of hunting, pointing retrievers, like the GSPs of today.

Campaigning against a faction which bred primarily for looks, stood the strong Dr Paul Kleeman, who was backed by an equally strong group of fundamentalists. They held to the 'through performance to type' dogma. In other words, they looked for perfection of performance, and the temperament and physique was so dictated that it enabled the dog to perform most

ABOVE: Gessler, Pia Altenbach and Bella Altenbach, depicted in their homeland, 1897.

RIGHT: Morna, 1899.

efficiently and with the most style. That was the policy which the German breeders followed – and, indeed, they do so today. The policy of the German breed club is to ensure that only sufficiently good specimens are used for breeding, and that the stringent requirements of field tests and trials outweigh those of the show-ring.

The real development of the Shorthair in Germany was naturally severely endangered by the 1939-45 war. Recovery was not simple afterwards, due to the splitting asunder of the German nation into East and West Germany, divided by the principle and the brickwork of the Berlin Wall. Only time will tell what part the Germans will play in the future development of the breed. Oddly enough, it would appear that the German approach to the assessment of quality in dogs differs somewhat from that accepted in almost all the other countries of my experience. On the occasions when I have been an exhibitor under German judges at shows in the UK, their deliberations have always been a mystery to me and to many of my co-exhibitors – though, naturally we accepted their opinion, as that was the reason for entering under them. Alternatively, the German regulations, requirements and procedures for field trials are sophisticated in the extreme.

A Swiss postcard, dated 1916, depicting a hunter with his three German Shorthaired Pointers.

Large numbers of dogs compete at all levels of field work tests and the title of 'Sieger' (Field Champion) is not easily attained. In several countries of Europe there are Championship shows and some field trials open to international competition. British quarantine laws exclude United Kingdom owners from competition; but Italian, Dutch, Austrian, French and Scandinavian dogs compete with German dogs, as there are no travel restrictions to or from those countries.

Today, some hundred years after the founding of the first breed club, the Shorthair has become an internationally known gundog. The individual dogs belong, undoubtedly, to the same breed, whichever country they are in, and their work schedule encompasses the same purpose. Nevertheless, there is sufficient individuality in each country to merit separate consideration. It is interesting to consider the varying factors which create the differences, while, at the same time, recognising the basic requirements which ensure that the GSP remains the same all-purpose sporting dog, regardless of the continent in which it is encountered.

Chapter Two

ACQUIRING YOUR GSP

MAKING THE CHOICE
The reasons for purchasing a GSP are various, and motives may differ for people according to their needs. Whether the desire is just to have a dog in the family, and consideration of the options leads you to choose the GSP, or the requirement is specifically to have an all-purpose gundog, matters little. The fact is that if the decision has been made to acquire a German Shorthaired Pointer, then it is wise to survey the market options.

It cannot be too strongly advised that you should buy an eight-to-ten-week-old, well-bred puppy to raise and train in your own way. Taking on someone else's adult dog can pose all sorts of unnecessary hazards, and is not worth the risk if you are intent on having a really well-socialised dog. Dogs from rescue organisations do sometimes turn out to be satisfactory, of course, but they do not always do so, nor do they usually have registration papers. That is not to say that you should not send your young dog away for training by a professional when old enough, if you can afford to do so and do not feel competent to do the job yourself. But in that event you have to remember that the dog is not a machine to be switched on and off and the changeover from trainer to owner can be difficult. There is no evidence to suggest that gundogs have to work in their traditional role to lead happy lives. If that was so, then the thousands of gundogs which are trained as guide dogs for blind people would be unhappy and frustrated. But GSPs do have a big capacity for learning, in addition to boundless energy. If these factors are not directed into some satisfying activity, then the owner will assuredly have a problem dog. GSPs do not live happily if restricted to life in a block of high-rise flats. They are not suitable pets for those who cannot give them adequate exercise, and they certainly benefit from some degree of training and discipline.

FINDING THE RIGHT DOG
There is little to be gained by buying a cheap dog from a questionable source. Once your GSP becomes part of the family, not only will the dog's breeding begin to show in both temperament and trainability, but the healthiest, happiest and best-bred dog in the world will cost no more to feed than the inferior one. A top-quality dog makes no more visits to the vet, and does not disrupt the family any more or less than the most veritable mongrel. A well-bred GSP puppy, with a qualified working background, is the most likely to be a satisfactory addition to the household. Naturally, German Pointers are best owned, trained and used in the field by rough-shooting enthusiasts. In parallel with that existence, they can be a most rewarding and delightful companion for the sportsman and his family. The GSP's nature allows these dogs to be a continuing source of delight and pleasure to young and old alike.

German Shorthaired Pointers are highly intelligent dogs, with boundless energy.

Nash.

When buying your GSP, therefore, take a look at what the market offers and do a spot of investigative homework before making a decision. The breed clubs can offer advice about availability, but do not expect them to make a final choice for you. Those interested enough can study the recorded successes of the different breeders and their bloodlines by reference to the Kennel Club Stud Book, which lists all the dogs who have won awards in Field Trials and major awards in the show ring. Looking at the records over the years gives an informative insight into which breeders produce high-quality winning stock, year after year.

Contact breeders who advertise puppies or who have made plans to produce a litter. By arrangement, go and see the puppies as well as the adult dogs. The parents of the litter are likely to give a good indication of what you can expect of the puppies. If you are interested in good working stock, go and watch a few Field Trials where you will be able to see dogs demonstrating their worth, or ask a potential breeder to show you the prospective brood bitch working. Do not necessarily accept the assurance of the vendor that the bitch in question 'does it all perfectly'! You will also need to consider the quality of the sire, although you will find that reputable breeders with good working stock rarely mate their bitches to unproven sires.

Assessing a six-week-old puppy: When you choose a puppy, it should be clean, well-cared-for, with a nice, extrovert character.

Sh.Ch. Barleyarch Panther, bred and owned by Martin and Sue Harris. The male is an impressive-looking animal, and may have that extra bit of drive compared with a bitch.

Do not feel bound to make a choice from any litter because you have been to see it. Only buy when you are happy that you are getting exactly what you want. If the home, the kennel and the conditions in which the puppies and other dogs are kept is not as you would like, do not buy a puppy. Invariably, good quality and well-reared puppies come from good homes. However, the pitfalls are not as numerous as you might imagine, and providing you ensure that you are dealing with reputable breeders, there is little likelihood of experiencing problems.

CHOOSING THE SEX

The choice of dog or bitch puppy can only be made by the individual. Many people find bitches more loving and perhaps slightly more biddable. Conversely, others look for that extra bit of drive, and appreciate the sheer masculinity displayed by many male dogs. Remember that dogs are distracted by bitches – very much so if they are on heat. Alternatively, bitches do come into season twice a year and during that state have to be kept safe from dogs; they may not act normally as far

Maureen Nixon's bitch Ch. Quintanna Tyr: The bitch is lovable and biddable in training.

as work goes and are restricted from field competition in order not to distract the male dog competitors. In the UK there are no restrictions on taking a bitch in season to a dog show, though the presence of one can cause havoc among the dogs, particularly if they are experienced at stud. It seems to be very unsporting to ignore a bitch's season and to go dog-showing regardless. You may find that your bitch will need more gentle handling than a dog, but GSPs are sensitive animals, at least the best of them are, and both sexes will generally be equally biddable.

PLACING AN ORDER

Most breeders like to have firm orders, backed up with a written letter and a deposit against the purchase price of the puppy, that should be conveyed when the puppy is collected. Arrange to take your puppy home as near to eight weeks of age as possible. The sooner the pup can settle into the new life ahead, the easier it will be, but GSPs are not normally ready to leave the nest much before that age.

COLLECTING THE PUPPY

Make certain that your puppy has been registered with the Kennel Club (or that the registration is in progress), and obtain from the breeder some instructions on feeding and a copy of the pedigree. You will also need to ascertain what inoculations, if any, your puppy has had, plus details of the worming programme. If you have to make a journey by car, it is desirable to have someone with you to look after the puppy. Come equipped with a blanket for warmth, and also some newspapers for use in the event of a 'mishap' on the journey. Bear in mind that this is a traumatic event for the puppy who will never have been away from the rest of the litter. This is the time to begin establishing the relationship between you and the puppy which is so essential to successful dog training. From the very first minute you can demonstrate your love and care, which your puppy will soon come to trust and reciprocate. The essential factors for the puppy's well-being are warmth, a sense of security, and adequate food.

SETTLING IN

There is always a danger of falling between two stools in the initial period of the puppy being with you. The puppy certainly will not be happy shut out in a kennel, feeling lonely, afraid and cold. But neither will future happiness for either of you result from letting your new friend sleep on your bed! It is certainly recommended that a GSP puppy should be part of the family, but the pup's place in the family 'pack' should be clearly defined. Give your GSP a chance to settle down in the new surroundings, and you soon find that all pups are happier with a disciplined routine.

Your puppy will appreciate regular feeding (in accordance with the breeder's instructions), and a warm, dry place to sleep in and rest undisturbed. Puppies do little but sleep, eat, relieve themselves, and play. For the latter activity your pup will like a few toys, the odd old slipper, a hard 'chew' and a ball perhaps; but most of all your puppy will appreciate human company. Spend time with your pup, playing learning games, but not beyond the extent of a youngster's limited concentration. Do everything you can to gain your puppy's trust and affection; the success of these first few weeks will be reflected in your GSP's biddability in the forthcoming months.

VETERINARY EXAMINATION

Within a day or so of getting home with your new acquisition, it is advisable to make contact with your local vet and arrange to take your pup for an examination. The vet will be able to confirm that the puppy is in good health and not suffering from any untoward condition. If by any chance the examination shows that there is something wrong with the puppy, you are entitled, within your rights as a purchaser, to return the puppy, most preferably with a letter from the vet, and to be reimbursed.

FEEDING

Follow the advice of the breeder, but remember that as your puppy grows, more and more food will be required. GSPs are usually good eaters and although the baby will not eat huge quantities at each meal, a young, growing dog will eventually need up to three or four times the protein intake of an adult dog. We find the use of a high quality 'complete food' to be ideal. Your puppy will need to eat four times a day initially, consuming an increasing quantity of food as the weeks go by. This should be reduced to three meals daily at about sixteen weeks and down to two meals at nine months or so.

Many people feed adult dogs only once a day. I have found from experience that dogs are happier and healthier if fed twice daily. I advise feeding a small meal at breakfast time and a larger one at about six o'clock in the evening. The general health of your dog will be reflected in the faeces; if your dog tends to diarrhoea, the dog is either unwell or the diet is unsuitable.

WORMING
Almost all puppies have roundworms. Even if the bitch was properly wormed and the puppies were treated by the breeder, there is still every chance that some will still be present in your puppy at ten or twelve weeks. Modern science has made their eradication simple, however, and your vet will be able to provide you with suitable medication. Follow the instructions carefully. It may be necessary to repeat the treatment a month later, or even several times in the first twelve months of your puppy's life.

INOCULATIONS AND VACCINATIONS
In various parts of the world there are regulations regarding treatment to guard against different diseases and worm infestations. They should be carefully observed. It is also essential to have your puppy immunised against the quite common but often deadly ailments, such as distemper, hepatitis and parvo-virus. Cleanliness of body and bedding, fresh air, exercise and good food, are the essentials to accompany good health – just as much for dogs as for humans.

BOARDING KENNELS
There is likely to be a time when you want or need to go away from home without your dog. It is not advisable to put puppies under six months of age into boarding kennels, indeed most kennel proprietors would not take them, but otherwise there is no reason whatever why your youngster should not go to kennels for a few weeks.

Most boarding kennels are strictly controlled by local authorities, but in any event, they are owned by experienced and caring dog owners. At any good establishment you will be welcome to go and inspect the kennels before you make a reservation for your dog, but think of it as sending your pet to a holiday camp, rather than to a prison. Having kept a kennel for twenty years, I am sure that dogs come to no harm, and mostly really do enjoy their 'holiday'. The professional kennel owner will be much more competent to look after your 'treasure' than an eager but ill-equipped neighbour, friend or relative.

EXERCISE
Young dog needs out-door exercise. It does not matter if it is raining and your GSP gets wet, providing that you towel and dry your puppy properly when you come back. If it is exceptionally cold while you are out, see that your puppy gets plenty of exercise to keep warm. If you let your puppy out alone, you must ensure that it is into a totally enclosed and safe area. However, both you and your pup will benefit from taking exercise together! The basic puppy training lessons can be started as soon as you feel that your puppy accepts you as a friend, but keep the sessions brief and simple. Make every game a lesson, and every lesson a game, but do not expect your puppy to get everything right first time.

REGISTRATION
When you receive the KC registration papers from the breeder, your puppy will be registered as being owned by the breeder, not by you. The details of re-registering are on the form and it is advisable to change the registered ownership to yourself. This is desirable in any case, but it is very necessary if you subsequently breed with your GSP.

Chapter Three

THE BREED STANDARD

DRAWING UP A STANDARD

The Breed Standard is a written blueprint to describe the ideal dog. A separate Standard exists for every recognised pure breed of dog. Each one, necessarily, is unique to the breed it represents. It is the pattern, the picture, the assembly instructions, the written word, which, if correctly interpreted, tells the reader what the finished product should look like, and to some extent, how it should behave! One of the real problems with Breed Standards is that, because they are only words, they are open to variety of interpretation. Even if the words are specific in some detail (as with size in the German Shorthaired Pointer Standard), they give some bracket which allows for variation within limits. Extraordinarily enough, even those brackets are sometimes ignored by breeders – either because they fail to breed to the specific requirement, or they choose to 'know better' than the pioneers who developed the breed.

Many writers have made a big issue of comparing the Standards, which vary slightly in different countries, all applying to German Shorthaired Pointers. There seems to be little point in this exercise. There are three GSP Standards in the world, but the fact is that (with a few exceptions) they are all intended to be the same. The first Standard for the GSP was, naturally enough, written and accepted by those people who were responsible for the emergence of the breed, i.e. the breed fanciers of Germany. Because the typically teutonic approach to everything is thorough, their Standard is 'wordy'. It comments in great detail on many aspects, and it includes a list of major and minor faults. It was, of course, written in German. The Federation Cynologique Internationale (FCI), the international canine body based in Belgium, accepted the German Standard and translated it into several European languages, and it is now the Standard of all the countries in Europe with the exception of the UK.

The Shorthair gained sufficient popularity to be accepted as a registered breed in the United States of America in 1930 (about five years after the first arrivals), long before it 'arrived' in any other English-speaking country; and the American owners, in collaboration, no doubt, with the AKC, produced their acceptable translation of the German Standard. They had no desire to alter the breed, and their translation was, in effect, accurate, but perhaps more succinct. The same thing happened in due course in Great Britain. Soon after the end of the 1939-45 war, a new group of enthusiastic owners consulted with the Kennel Club, looked at the American Standard, and translated the German version. Their deliberations resulted in the emergence of the third Standard for the breed, which, modified slightly since in wording, in line with all British Standards, is now adopted in South Africa, New Zealand and Australia. The American version is used in Canada, and most other countries in the world have adopted the German/FCI version.

Am. Ch. Tabor's Don't Think Twice Dylan. The German Shorthaired Pointer should give the impression of a noble, well-balanced animal.

THE AMERICAN BREED STANDARD

The Shorthair is a versatile hunter, an all-purpose gundog capable of high performance in field and water. The judgement of Shorthairs in the show-ring should reflect this basic characteristic.

GENERAL APPEARANCE
The overall picture which is created in the observer's eye, is that of an aristocratic, well-balanced, symmetrical animal, with conformation indicating power, endurance and agility and a look of intelligence and animation. The dog is neither small nor conspicuously large. It gives the impression of medium size, but is like the proper hunter (hunter in this context refers to a horse used for hunting with pack-hounds), with a short back, but standing over plenty of ground.

Tall leggy dogs, or dogs which are ponderous or unbalanced because of excess substance should be definitely rejected. The first impression is that of keenness, which denotes full enthusiasm for work without indication of nervous or flighty character. Movements are alertly co-ordinated without waste motion. Grace of outline, clean-cut head, sloping shoulders, deep chest, powerful back, strong quarters, good bone composition, adequate muscle, well-carried tail and taut coat, all combine to produce a look of nobility and an indication of anatomical structure essential to correct gait which must indicate a heritage of purposefully conducted breeding. Doggy bitches and bitchy dogs are to be faulted. A judge must excuse a dog from the ring if it displays extreme shyness or viciousness towards its handler or the judge. Aggressiveness or belligerence toward another dog is not to be considered viciousness.

SYMMETRY
Symmetry and field quality are most essential. A dog in hard and lean field condition is not to be penalized. However, overly fat or poorly muscled dogs are to be penalized. A dog well-balanced in all points is preferable to one with outstanding good qualities and defects.

HEAD
Clean-cut, neither too light nor too heavy, in proper proportion to the body. Skull is reasonably broad, arched on the side and slightly round on top. Scissura (median line between the eyes and the forehead) not too deep, occipital bone not as conspicuous as in the case of the Pointer. The foreface rises gradually from nose to forehead. The rise is more pronounced in the dog than in the bitch as befitting his sex. The chops fall away from the somewhat projecting nose. Lips are full and deep, never flewy. The chops do not fall over too much, but form a proper fold in the angle. The jaw is powerful and the muscles well-developed. The line to the forehead rises gradually and never has a definite stop as that of the Pointer, but rather a stop effect when viewed from the side, due to the position of the eyebrows. The muzzle is sufficiently long to enable the dog to seize properly and to facilitate his carrying game a long time. A pointed muzzle is not desirable. The entire head never gives the impression of tapering to a point. The depth is in the right proportion to the length, both in the muzzle and in the skull proper. The length of the muzzle should equal the length of the skull. A pointed muzzle is a fault. A dish-faced muzzle is a fault. Too many wrinkles in the forehead is a fault.

The GSP's eyes should be full of intelligence and expressive, good-humoured and yet radiating energy.

Nash.

EYES
The eyes are of medium size, full of intelligence and expressive, good humoured and yet radiating energy, neither protruding nor sunken. The eye is almond shaped, not circular. The eyelids close well. The best color is dark brown. Light yellow (Bird of Prey) eyes are not desirable and are a fault. Closely set eyes are to be faulted. China or wall eyes are to be disqualified.

NOSE
Brown, the larger the better, nostrils well-opened and broad. Spotted nose not desirable. Flesh colored nose disqualifies.

TEETH
The teeth are strong and healthy. The molars inter-mesh properly. The bite is a true scissors bite. A perfect level bite (without overlapping) is not desirable and must be penalized. Extreme overshot or undershot bite disqualifies.

NECK
Of proper length to permit the jaws reaching game to be retrieved, sloping downwards on beautiful curving lines. The nape is rather muscular, becoming gradually larger towards the shoulders. Moderate hound-like throatiness permitted.

CHEST
The chest in general gives the impression of depth rather than breadth; for all that, it should be in correct proportion to the other parts of the body with a fair depth. The chest reaches down to the elbows, the ribs forming the thorax show a rib spring and are not flat or slab-sided; they are not perfectly round or barrel-shaped. Ribs that are entirely round prevent the necessary expansion of the chest when taking breath. The back ribs reach well down. The circumference of the thorax immediately behind the elbows is smaller than that of the thorax about a hand's-breadth behind elbows, so that the upper arm has room for movement.

BACK, LOINS AND CROUP
Back is short, strong and straight with a slight rise from root of tail to withers. Loin strong, of moderate length and slightly arched. Tuck-up is apparent. Excessively long, roach or swayed back must be penalized.

FOREQUARTERS
The shoulders are sloping, movable, well-covered with muscle. The shoulder blades lie flat and are well laid back nearing a 45 degree angle. The upper arm (the bones between the shoulder and elbow joints) is as long as possible, standing away somewhat from the trunk so that the straight and closely muscled legs, when viewed from the front, appear to be parallel.

Elbows which stand away from the body or are too close indicate toes turning inwards or outwards, which must be regarded as faults. Pasterns are strong, short and nearly vertical with a slight spring. Loose, short-bladed or straight shoulders must be faulted. Down in the pasterns is to be faulted.

HINDQUARTERS
The hips are broad with hip sockets wide apart and fall slightly towards the tail in a graceful curve.

Thighs are strong, well-muscled. Stifles well bent. Hock joints are well angulated and strong, straight bone structure from hock to pad. Angulation of both stifle and hock joint is such as to combine maximum combination of both drive and traction. Hocks turn neither in nor out. A steep croup is a fault. Cow-hocked legs are a serious fault.

FEET
Are compact, close-knit, and round to spoon-shaped. The toes sufficiently arched and heavily nailed. The pads are strong, hard and thick. Dewclaws on the hind legs must be removed. Dewclaws on the forelegs may be removed. Feet pointing in or out is a fault.

COAT AND SKIN
The skin is close and tight. The hair is short and thick and feels tough to the hand; it is somewhat longer on the under-side of the tail and the back edges of the haunches. It is softer, thinner and shorter on the ears and the head. Any dog with long hair in body coat is to be severely penalized.

TAIL
Is set high and firm, and must be docked leaving 40 per cent of length. The tail hangs down when the dog is quiet, is held horizontally when he is walking. The tail must never be curved over the back towards the head when the dog is moving. A tail curved or bent towards the head is to be severely penalized.

BONES
Thin and fine bones are by no means desirable in a dog which must possess strength and be able to work over any and every country. The main importance accordingly is laid not so much on the size of bones, but rather on their being in proper proportion to the body. Bone structure too heavy or too light is a fault. Dogs with coarse bones are handicapped in agility of movement and speed.

WEIGHT AND HEIGHT
Dogs, 55 to 70 pounds (25 to 31.8 kgs).
Bitches, 45 to 60 pounds (20.4 to 27.2 kgs).
Dogs, 23 to 25 inches (58.4 to 63.5 cms) at the withers.
Bitches, 21 to 23 inches (53.3 to 58.4 cms) at the withers.
Deviations of 1 inch (2.5 cms) over or above the described heights are to be severely penalized.

COLOR
The coat may be solid liver or any combination of liver and white such as liver and white ticked, liver spotted and white ticked, or liver roan. A dog with any area of black, red, orange, lemon or tan or a dog solid white will be disqualified.

GAIT
A smooth, light gait is essential. It is to be noted that as gait increases from the walk to a faster speed, the legs converge beneath the body. The tendency to single track is desirable. The forelegs reach well ahead as if to pull in the ground without giving the appearance of a hackney gait, and are followed by the back legs which give forceful propulsion. Dragging the rear feet is undesirable.

DISQUALIFICATIONS
China or wall eyes.
Flesh colored nose.
Extreme overshot or undershot.
A dog with any area of black, red, orange, lemon, or tan, or a dog solid white.

Reproduced by kind permission of the American Kennel Club.

THE FCI AND GERMAN BREED STANDARD

GENERAL APPEARANCE
The general appearance is that of an aristocratic, harmonious dog with a conformation which guarantees endurance, power and agility. This is further expressed through his noble appearance, the grace of outline, the clean-cut, dry head, well carried tail and taut shiny coat.

SIZE
Dogs, 62 to 66 cms. measured at the withers. Bitches, 58 to 63 cms. measured at the withers.

HEAD
Dry, clean-cut lines, neither too light nor too heavy, length and size in proportion to the body. The skull should be reasonably broad, slightly arched, the medial furrow (median line between the eyes at the forehead) not too deep. The nasal bridge, viewed in profile, should rise in an aristocratic slight Roman nose or a slight rise above a straight line. Still acceptable is a straight nasal bridge, a dish-faced nose is undesirable. The lips fall away from the somewhat protruding nose and then continue in a flat, beautifully shaped curve to the corners of the mouth. The lips should not hang over too much. The chops are strong with well-developed muscles. The line to the forehead rises gradually. The eyebrows, viewed from the side, form a definite stop. The muzzle must be strong and long in order to facilitate the seizing and carrying of wild game.

EARS
Moderately long, neither too fleshy nor too fine, broad and high set, lie flat to the head without twisting, rounded at the bottom. The ears, when pulled to the front, should reach the corners of the mouth.

EYES
Of medium size, neither protruding nor too deep set. The eye lids close well. The preferred colour is dark brown.

NOSE
Brown; nostrils well opened, broad, movable. A flesh-coloured or spotted nose is undesirable and is only permissible with the white base coat colour.

TEETH
Strong, preferably complete dentition and correct positioning of teeth: i.e. the P4 of the upper jaw should over-reach the M1 and M2 of the lower jaw. The premolars of the upper and lower jaw are

alternately situated. The incisors should form a scissors bite. The incisors of the upper jaw should not protrude more than 2 mm. over those of the lower jaw.

NECK
Of good length in proportion to the body structure, very muscular, slightly arched, gradually broadening towards the shoulders. The skin at the throat should be as tight as possible.

CHEST AND RIBCAGE
The chest in general gives the impression of depth rather than breadth, for all that it should be in correct proportion to the other parts of the body. With proper length of the upper arm, the breast bone should reach to the height of the elbow joint. The thorax should be of good length with a well developed forechest, and should form a pleasing, gradual curve toward the loin area. A recessed chest is undesirable. The ribs forming the thorax should be well curved and should not be flat (like those of the Greyhound), nor round nor barrel-shaped. Ribs that are entirely round prevent the necessary expansion of chest when breathing. The last ribs reach well down.

BACK, LOINS, BODY, CROUP
A strong back is particularly important for rapid movement and endurance. Therefore it should not be too long, and the loins should be broad and elastic as well as straight to slightly arched. The spinal process of the dorsal vertebrae should be well covered by muscles. The croup should be broad and sufficiently long, not steep, starting at the height of the level back and only slightly sloping towards the tail. There should be a slight tuck-up in order to provide adequate room while galloping; without giving the impression of being thin-bodied.

FOREQUARTERS
The shoulders should be sloping, dry and well muscled. The shoulder blades should lie flat. The upper arm should be as long as possible. The elbow joint should lie far back and be neither tight nor turned outward. The lower arms should be straight sufficiently muscled with strong, yet not thick or coarse bones. The pastern joint should be slightly angulated and the pastern should never be straight to the ground.

HINDQUARTERS
The pelvic area should be long, broad and roomy. The upper thigh should be broad and well muscled, the lower thighs and metatarsus correctly angulated: over angulation affects the endurance. The hocks should be strong. Viewed from the rear they should be straight or slightly turned outward under the hock joints. Dewclaws must be removed because they hinder the dog.

FEET
Strong and compact, round to oval. Well-arched toes with strong nails. the pads should be strong and hard.

COAT
The skin should be tight without any wrinkles. The coat is short and dense and should be tough and harsh to the touch. At the ears and head it is shorter and thinner; on the underside of the tail it should not be noticeably longer.

TAIL
High set, strong at the base then tapering; of medium length; however, to avoid injury it should be docked to one half its length. In repose the tail hangs down, it is held horizontally when the dog is walking; it should not be carried too high or curved over the back: vigorously wagging while on the search.

BONES
Thin, fine bones are not desirable in a dog which must be able to work in all types of terrain. However, it is not the size of the bones which is essential but rather the composition or density of the bones. Dogs with coarse bones are handicapped in agility of movement and speed.

COLOUR
The permissible colours are:
a. Liver without markings.
b. Liver with some white spots or ticking on the chest and legs.
c. Dark roan, with brown head, brown patches or spots. The base colour of such dogs is not brown with white or white with brown, but the hair shows such an intensive mixing of brown and white that the exterior will have the valuable camouflaged appearance which is so practical for use. At the inner part of the hind legs, as well as the tip of the tail, the colouring is often lighter. The colour of the head is usually brown; often, however, one finds a ticked nasal bridge and occiput as well as speckled flews.
d. Light roan with a brown head, brown patches or spots. With this colouring, brown is found in lesser quantity, the white hair is predominant; therefore dogs of this colour generally appear lighter.
e. White, with brown markings on the head, large brown patches or spots on the body.
f. Black in the same colour patterns as brown or roan. Sharp reddish yellow markings (brand) are permissible.
Dogs without docked tails and with dewclaws must be disqualified since they do not represent the Standard.

Reproduced by kind permission of the Federation Cynologique Internationale.

THE BRITISH BREED STANDARD

GENERAL APPEARANCE
Noble, steady dog showing power, endurance and speed, giving the immediate impression of an alert and energetic dog whose movements are well co-ordinated. Of medium size, with a short back standing over plenty of ground. Grace of outline, clean-cut head, long sloping shoulders, deep chest, short back, powerful hindquarters, good bone composition, adequate muscle, well carried tail and taut coat.

CHARACTERISTICS
Dual purpose Pointer/Retriever, very keen nose, perseverance in searching and initiative in game-finding, excellence in field, a naturally keen worker, equally good on land and water.

TEMPERAMENT
Gentle, affectionate and even-tempered. Alert, biddable and very loyal.

HEAD AND SKULL.
Clean-cut, neither too light nor too heavy, well proportioned to body. Skull sufficiently broad and slightly round. Nasal bone rising gradually from nose to forehead (this is more pronounced in dogs) and never possessing a definite stop, but when viewed from the side a well defined stop effect due to position of eyebrows. Lips falling away almost vertically from somewhat protruding nose and continuing in a slight curve to corner of mouth. Lips well developed, not over hung. Jaws powerful and sufficiently long to enable the dog to pick up and carry game. Dish-faced and snipy muzzle undesirable. Nose solid brown or black depending on coat colour. Wide nostrils, well opened and soft.

EYES
Medium size, soft and intelligent, neither protruding nor too deep set. Varying in shades of brown to tone with coat. Light eye undesirable. Eyelids should close properly.

EARS
Broad and set high; neither too fleshy nor too thin, with a short, soft coat; hung close to head, no pronounced fold, rounded at tip and reaching almost to corner of mouth when brought forward.

MOUTH
Teeth sound and strong. Jaws strong, with a perfect regular and complete scissor bite, i.e. upper teeth closely overlapping lower teeth and set square to the jaws.

NECK
Moderately long, muscular and slightly arched, thickening towards the shoulders. Skin not fitting too loosely.

FOREQUARTERS
Shoulders sloping and very muscular, top of shoulder blades close; upper arm bones, between shoulder and elbow, long. Elbows well laid back, neither pointing outwards nor inwards. Forelegs straight and lean, sufficiently muscular and strong, but not coarse-boned. Pasterns slightly sloping.

BODY
Chest must appear deep rather than wide but in proportion to rest of body; ribs deep and well sprung, never barrel-shaped nor flat; back ribs reaching well down to tuck up of loins. Chest measurement immediately behind elbows smaller than about a hand's breadth behind elbows so that upper arm has freedom of movement. Firm, short back, not arched. Loin wide and slightly arched; croup wide and sufficiently long, neither too heavy nor too sloping starting on a level with back and sloping gradually towards tail. Bones solid and strong. Skin should not fit loosely or fold.

HINDQUARTERS
Hips broad and wide falling slightly towards tail. Thighs strong and well muscled. Stifles well bent. Hocks square with body and slightly bent, turning neither in nor out. Pasterns nearly upright.

FEET
Compact, close knit, round to spoon shaped, well padded, turning neither in nor out. Toes well arched with strong nails.

TAIL
Starts high and thick growing gradually thinner, customarily docked to medium length by two-fifths to half its length. When quiet, tail carried down; when moving, horizontally; never held high over back or bent.

GAIT/MOVEMENT
Smooth lithe gait essential. As gait increases from walk to a faster speed, legs converge beneath body (single tracking). Forelegs reach well ahead, effortlessly covering plenty of ground with each stride and followed by hindlegs which give forceful propulsion.

COAT
Short, flat and coarse to touch, slightly longer under tail.

COLOUR
Solid liver, liver and white spotted, liver and white spotted and ticked, liver and white ticked, solid black or black and white same variations (not tri-colour).

SIZE
Dogs minimum height 58 cms (23 ins) at withers, maximum height 64 cms (25 ins) at withers. Bitches minimum height 53 cms (21 ins) at withers, maximum height 59 cms (23 ins) at withers.

FAULTS
Any departure from the foregoing points should be considered a fault and the seriousness with which the fault should be regarded should be in exact proportion to its degree.

NOTE
Male animals should have two apparently normal testicles fully descended into the scrotum.

Reproduced by kind permission of the English Kennel Club.

CONSIDERING THE STANDARDS
Apart from the fact that the British Standard is so much more succinct, there are few differences, though often lengthy attempts at description fail to be any clearer in meaning. A detailed study of the three Standards will show how similar they all are – in intent, if not in actual words. There is nothing to be gained by looking for word differences in the three Standards in order to see great variety of type in different countries. The German Shorthaired Pointer, the Shorthair, the GSP, the Kurzhaar – all are the same breed type. There never has been any intention to change the Standard in principle, with two exceptions, colour and size (height), which we should consider separately.

The fact is that, despite the general acceptance of the Standard, some breeders choose to ignore aspects of it. They breed dogs, for one reason or another, which flout the obvious intention of the

Points Of Anatomy

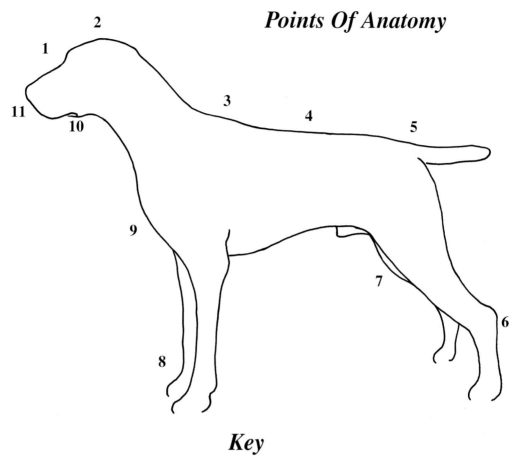

Key

1. Stop
2. Occiput
3. Withers
4. Back
5. Croup
6. Hock

7. Stifle
8. Pastern
9. Fore chest
10. Flews
11. Muzzle

wording. One simple example has to be that of tail carriage of almost all Shorthairs in the show-ring, and more particularly of the field dogs in the United States of America. Tradition, and that is the only thing to account for it, dictates that pointing breeds, whether tail-docked or not, should stand at the point with a high tail carriage, presumably to be more clearly visible.

Strangely, it never happened in Europe, or Great Britain, though there is a noticeable swing in that direction in Australia. GSPs are often exhibited in that country with their tails pushed up to a vertical position and 'choked up' like one might expect to see a Dobermann or Boxer. I have many times asked handlers in Australia why they do this, being in strict contravention of the Standard.

Skeleton

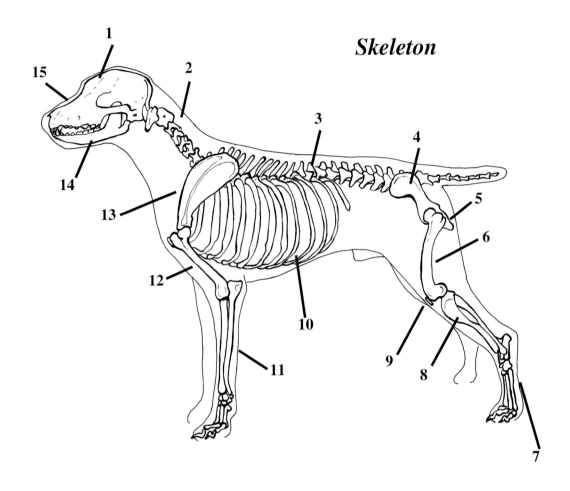

Key

1. Skull
2. Neck (Cervical vertebrae)
3. Back (Lumbar vertebrae)
4. Pelvic Bone
5. Hip Joint
6. Upper thigh (Femur)
7. Hock (Metatarsals)
8. Second thigh (Tibia/Fibula)
9. Patella
10. Ribs
11. Lower arm (Radius/Ulna)
12. Upper arm (Humerus)
13. Shoulder (Scapula)
14. Lower jaw
15. Upper jaw

'Oh, this is the only way to win under all-rounder judges', was the only answer I got!

Another example of divergence from the Standard is the type now being produced by some breeders in the Eastern States of Australia and New Zealand, where they appear to be following a fashion, perhaps first set by Weimaraner breeders. They are producing dogs with an excessively pronounced forechest and with extraordinarily long second thighs and exaggerated turn of stifle. The result is that soundness is lost. They are stacked with their hind feet so far behind their hips that they have to be supported in the show position by their tails, otherwise they collapse!

I can find no reason for this type, except that it accentuates the detail of the Standard both fore and aft. A close study of the Standard, and of top-winning correctly conformed dogs in the UK or Germany, will show that there is nothing 'over-done' relating to the German Pointer. If a dog looks exaggerated in any way, you can be sure it is faulty! Fortunately perhaps, it is generally the case in all dogdom that those breeders who choose to breed away from the Standard find, more often than not, that they are unsuccessful in show ring or field.

The following comments are intended to clarify some of the jargon and give a personal interpretation. It has to be remembered that these written words are all liable to variation of interpretation, and accents of importance are variously applied by individuals.

GENERAL APPEARANCE
All three Standards are agreed, and general appearance is accurately described. Even the use of the word 'medium' in relation to size, must be acceptable. Surely everyone has seen sufficient dogs to determine which are small, medium, large or gigantic?

CHARACTERISTICS
All agreed again. The British Standard calls for ability on land and water. Hopefully 'in' water is intended. Clever dogs they might be, but they do not walk on water!

HEAD AND SKULL
There is tremendous difficulty in accurately describing a head in a few words; so all the Standards lack completely positive definition. The call for balance with the body is universal.

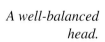

A well-balanced head.

FAULTY HEADS

Too heavy.

Lacking balance, weak lower jaw – probably overshot.

Too fine: lacking strength to carry game.

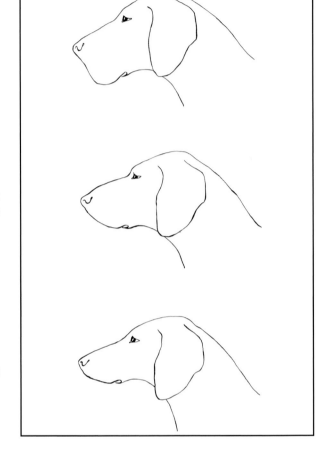

TEETH
The FCI Standard is positive with regard to complete dentition, and includes more detailed requirements than the American or British Standards.

Correct dentition: Complete scissor bite.

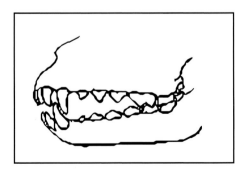

INCORRECT
DENTITION

Over-shot.

Under-shot.

Level bite.

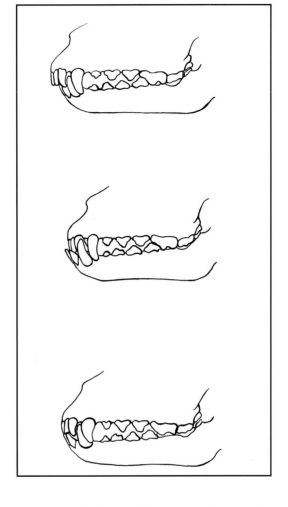

EARS
Because a great deal of a dog's character is expressed in the head, the eyes and ears are important to maintain type. Low-slung, ponderous ears give an untypical 'houndy' look, but small, very high set ears are equally wrong and give a terrier-like expression. Eyes are adequately described.

NECK
It is interesting that the FCI Standard calls for tight skin at the throat, the American allows moderate 'throatiness' and the British for skin 'not fitting too loosely'! I can only speculate as to how much accuracy is lost in translation.

FOREQUARTERS
This most important part of the physical construction of the dog materially affects its movement. A dog with shoulder blades lacking angulation cannot take 'daisy-cutting' long strides. The movement, therefore, is restricted to short steps or the pace is hackneyed, a method of front movement in which the foreleg is bent and held up while the body is propelled forward from the

rear. This is not desirable movement because it uses unnecessary energy. Also a dog with 'a good lay of shoulder' can more easily drop its head to the ground to pick up game. Because the greater portion of the dog's weight is carried by the front legs, poor construction in that quarter reduces the power of movement in every way.

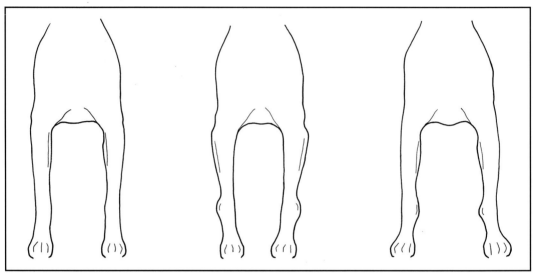

Correct front.   *Out at elbows.*   *Out-turned feet.*

SHOULDERS

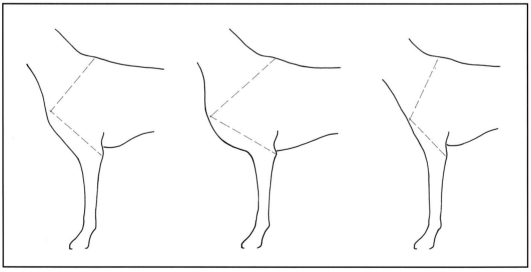

Correct:
good angulation.

Incorrect:
accentuated forechest.

Incorrect:
Straight in shoulder.

HINDQUARTERS

Looking at the Standards, it is clear that both fore and hind construction are closely linked with 'gait'. The major part of the propulsive power comes from the hindquarters of the dog. A dog without a turn of stifle and a short second thigh does not have the 'spring-like' power to propel the body forward, without dropping its hindquarters at every pace.

HINDQUARTERS

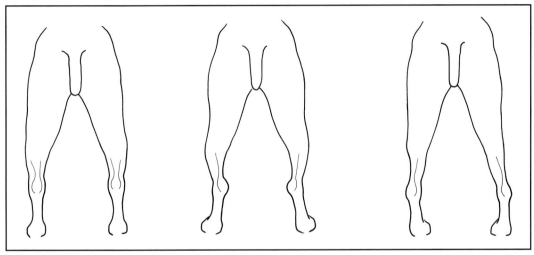

Correct.   *Incorrect: cow-hocks.*   *Incorrect: bow-legs.*

HINDQUARTERS ANGULATION

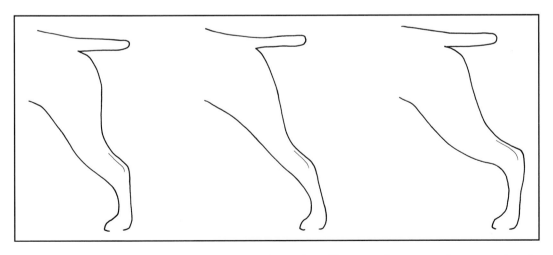

Correct.   *Incorrect: Straight stifle (short second thigh).*   *Incorrect: Over-angulated (second thigh is too long).*

FRONT ACTION

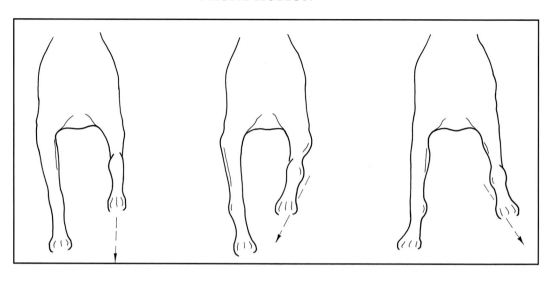

Correct.   Incorrect: Turned in.   Incorrect: Turned out.

HINDQUARTER DRIVE

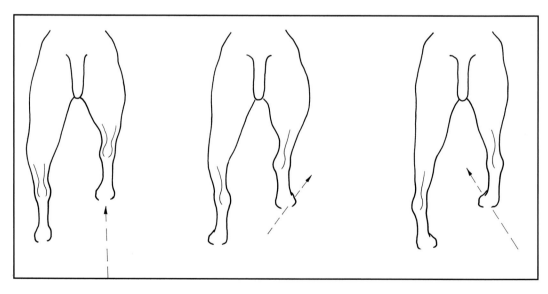

Correct: Power along   Incorrect: cow-hocks –   Incorrect: Turned out
line of direction.   wasted energy.   hocks – wasted energy.

Watch a 'straight behind' dog moving in the show-ring: you will see that its topline is going up and down with every step; whereas that of the properly proportioned dog is level, and it appears to move smoothly and effortlessly. This is a very important part of the construction of a dog which has to work for hours, as do hunting Shorthairs.

The quarters should be so constructed that the propulsive force given by the muscles is all directed along the line of movement. If a dog has cow hocks and turned out feet front and rear, then the propulsive power goes off at angles away from the the line of movement, and efficiency is reduced. This be seen most clearly by watching top-ranking human athletes running. Their movements show positively that all the effort is concentrated in the direction they are travelling, without energy-wasting flailing of arms or legs.

COAT
The coarseness called for in the coat is most noticeable when the dog is stroked against the 'nap'. It will feel quite bristly to the touch and very different from the average hound coat, which feels soft both ways. An over-long coat is inclined to wave along the back and to give feathers to the legs, which is not pretty or desirable.

COLOUR
The first of the exceptions to the equality of the three Standards exists with regard to colour in the American Standard. There is a good reason for the colour question, which can easily be explained. GSPs were originally liver and white, in all its variations, but in an attempt to darken eye colour, deliberate cross-mating was made to black Pointer blood. The result simply was that in addition to inheriting darker eyes, the breed also inherited the possibility for black and white coat colour, providing one of the parents was itself black/white.

This occurred in Germany, and for many years the black/white dogs were kept in a separate register from the liver/whites. As the American Standard was derived from the German original before blacks and livers were combined in one register, it excluded black/white. To date the AKC has not chosen to alter its Standard to accommodate black/white coated dogs. It is also a fact that the British Standard originally allowed liver/white only, but this was rectified several years ago to bring it in line with the German/FCI Standard, following the legitimate importation and breeding of black/white specimens.

The FCI Standard refers to 'brown' rather than 'liver'; again a matter of translation from one language to another. The coat, at best, should be the colour of cooked, rather than raw, liver. However, it should be noted that the coat often fades in the sun and immediately before moulting.

HEIGHT
The second variation relates to the question of size (height) in the German/ FCI Standard. No doubt the Germans had good reason, as they thought, to deliberately and materially alter the Standard which had stood sacrosanct for so many years, to increase the permitted height by about one inch. It could be argued that this was a short-sighted mistake.

Many breeds suffer from the problem of size, and for most dogs it is probably academic. Perhaps it is true that modern nutrition tends to produce bigger animals. Certainly the bigger 'good ones' fill the eye in the show-ring, particularly to the 'all-rounder' judge, and therefore tend to win. The winners, in turn, are more often used at stud or to breed from than the losers: and suddenly we are involved with breeding selectively for increased size – without even thinking about it.

Size is not, however, an insoluble problem In some breeds where it has been recognised that

Sven Rundberg's Ch. Randolph, pictured in Sweden. Tail docking is now banned in some countries, and this obviously has an influence on the general appearance and outline of the GSP.

over-size has become the accepted norm – the Chow Chow is one of them – selective breeding has been completely successful in returning the breed to the size called for in the Standard. For GSPs, size is particularly important. At some time in its working day, a GSP may be called upon to do the job of a Spaniel, flushing game out from close cover; and this is exactly why the requirement is for a medium-sized dog. But it is important to be reasonable in viewing this.

Certainly a Great Dane-sized dog cannot do the job of a Spaniel, but equally one inch up or down in the size of the individual dog is hardly likely to affect its work capability. It is the trend towards bigger and bigger dogs which presents the danger, and the broad principle should be to accept the Standard, and to endeavour to breed dogs which meet its requirements. There has to be some fault in the theory that the Standard is altered to match what is being bred. The remedy lies directly in the hands of judges in the show-ring.

If 23 inches is the minimum and 25 inches is the maximum for a male, then perfection must surely be at 24 inches. Regrettably, not one breeder in a hundred will accept this, and the general aim today is universally for the upper limit. The result is that at least 50 per cent of GSPs exhibited in the UK, and I suspect elsewhere, are over-size. This statement is made with personal conviction because, to the best of my knowledge, I am the only Championship Show judge to have measured them in the UK! I have done this on two occasions, about five years apart, purely to demonstrate the fact. At the second reckoning the figure was higher than at the first, but on neither occasion was even one of the exhibits under-size; even in the puppy classes.

FAULTS

The British Standard's comment on faults – that any departure from the points of the Standard 'should be considered a fault and the seriousness with which the fault should be regarded should be in exact proportion to its degree' – seems to be very comprehensive as an extension after any disqualifying faults. The addition of a requirement for all males to have two apparently normally descended testicles applies to British Standards for all breeds. It could well be adopted by other countries.

CONCLUSION

It is easy to criticise the Standard: many people do so. But it is obvious that without the Standard, we have no pattern against which to assess our dogs. Judges, breeders, and newcomers to the breed are all exhorted to read and digest the Standard, as being the way to understand and recognise the correct German Shorthaired Pointer. I am not absolutely sure that a minute study of the Standard alone, could make a person au fait with the breed; but it does enable everyone to have a common base on which to build knowledge.

The value of studying dogs as individuals and comparing one with another is only really given validity if it is done in conjunction with an understanding of the Standard. All judges worth their salt do it. Most 'all-rounder' gundog specialist judges, whether they admit it or not, carry a mental picture of the ideal GSP in their minds. That perfect picture is probably based on an interpretation of the Standard, and a memory of a dog they once saw, which, to their eyes, came nearest to perfection. When judging, they look for a specimen amongst those before them which most nearly meets their ideal. That is the one which wins first prize, and the one which looks most nearly like the winner, comes second, and so on.

What transpires, therefore, from a detailed consideration of the Standard is that it is a comprehensive and detailed way of describing the dog we should be looking for. It fails, of course, in regard to 'character', 'mental balance' and 'style'. These are enigmatic factors, not truly translatable into words. Dogs either have 'it', or they have not. Only experience enables us to see the character emanating from a dog – in just the same way as we recognise it in some human beings.

Chapter Four

BREEDING GSPs

BREEDING PRINCIPLES

OUT-CROSSING: There are several basic systems which can be used in breeding dogs. With 'out-crossing', true specimens of the breed are mated to one another, but every effort is made to ensure that there is no blood relationship between them, or if there is, it is only a distant one. It is the system usually dictated by society for the reproduction of the human species. It maintains vigour but does not strengthen family type.

LINE-BREEDING AND IN-BREEDING: The second of the options is called 'line-breeding'. Here, the chosen sire and dam will have some relationship to one another, though not necessarily a very close one. The final method is 'in-breeding', and in this system the sire and dam are deliberately chosen as mates because they do carry the same 'blood'. They may well be true brother/sister, mother/son or father/daughter matings.

MENDELIAN GENETICS

The object of using any of these systems is made clear by an understanding of the broadly accepted and applied theory originated by a scientist named Mendel. He made a close study of the fertilisation and growth of pulse vegetables and discovered that family type could be passed on from one generation to another. A simplified explanation of his theory is that any offspring (bean, flea, dog, human or whatever) inherit half of the gene make-up from the female producer and half from the male. So you and I got half of our genes – for which use the simpler words 'inherited characteristics' (for the one controls the other) – from our mother and half from our father, and therefore a quarter from each of our grandparents, an eighth from each great-grandparent and so on. This is true of all inborn characteristics both mental and physical, seen and unseen. Artistic leaning, the colour of eyes and skin, the shape of ears, the size of hands, feet, liver or kidneys, temperament and disposition – all were inherited from our parents. Now, if a brother/sister mating takes place, the offspring inherits doubled-up characteristics, because the inherited factors were common to both. This situation produces two results. One is that the characteristics (good and bad) are magnified in the offspring, and the other is that the offspring's own ability to pass on those characteristics is strengthened – termed 'prepotency'. This is very much a simplification of the technical jargon and facts, but it is still the basic truth, if you accept Mendel's theory.

It is generally accepted that the result can be affected to some degree by environmental factors, but it cannot be eradicated. This has affected the selection of stock to some degree for the fixing of type in breeding of almost all domestic and farm animals, including pedigree dogs, for many years. It is all a matter of degree. If you 'in-breed', the result is very strong type, but the magnified characteristics may show up as bad ones. Mendel also found that if in-breeding was repeated through several generations, size was reduced accompanied by the emergence of all sorts of undesirable traits. We can therefore assume that in-breeding is not a road to be travelled lightly.

THE ADVANTAGES OF LINE BREEDING

Line-breeding entails the mating of family-related animals, but not as closely related as in-breeding. Applied with consideration and selectivity, it can and does strengthen the type for which you are breeding. The system gives a strong family type and, with selection in the breeding programme, enables the breeder to eventually produce better dogs through the generations. Such a concentration of type cannot be the outcome of non-related matings, though often such out-crossing may be resorted to in an attempt to introduce a new and desirable characteristic into an established family line.

Not surprisingly therefore, a dog is normally only as good genetically as its parents. Sometimes, perhaps by a fluke combination of genes, a dog with the weakest of pedigrees turns out to be something better than ordinary. Usually the dog's attributes in such a case die with him: seldom does he prove to be a prepotent sire. Occasionally, bitches fail to relate in their producing capability to their own individual quality. This is almost invariably due to the oddity of their gene make-up. Conversely, with dogs and bitches which have consistently good 'blood' in their pedigrees: where their great-grandparents, grandparents, sire and dam have all proven their quality in the sphere they followed, and there is some relationship between them, then they have the chance to be good in that achievement and have the ability to pass their worth on to their own get.

Selective line-breeding to quality, tempered with the influx of new desirable blood when required or necessary, is the most likely way to produce quality stock. But even then, using a quality sire to an apparently suitable bitch, the results are never guaranteed. *Mistakenly, many people who own a mediocre bitch think that by paying for the service of a top sire they will be sure to produce top-quality offspring.* They waste years, and flood the market with less than desirable puppies in following such a plan. The way to produce consistently good stock is to mate only proven quality bitches to proven quality sires, and to select only the best of that stock for future breeding.

This does not always mean you should line-breed to the same family. It is true in principle that mating dogs of the same family, at least strengthens the family type; whereas complete out-crossing dilutes the family characteristics. But out-crossing a line-bred bitch of quality to another line-bred sire of quality, but of an entirely different family, often adds vigour to the blood and allows the offspring to inherit some desirable trait from the sire that was missing in the dam. In other words, it is a way of improving stock, which should be the considered aim of all breeders of GSPs. It is not enough to just want a replacement puppy, to use the nearest sire to hand and to sell the others of the litter to whoever comes along. Every mating of GSPs ever made should be with the intention of improving the stock of the breed – for the breed's sake, not for the breeder's.

There is little purpose in entering further into a discussion on genetics. Many detailed books have been written on the subject which are available to the enthusiast. It is a very complex subject, and, whatever is written, not all will agree. Many geneticists are at difference with one another; and who is to say for sure who is right and who is wrong? Nature is so fickle. She leads us up so many false trails. But, providing breeders grasp the very broad principle of breeding from, to and through quality, then the general standard within a breed will be maintained or improved.

Success does not come easily. If the breeding of top-quality dogs was simple, everyone would be

Carol Chadwick's Am. Can. Ch. NMK's Placer Country Snowbird: A top-producing sire with over forty Show Champions to his credit.

Bob Keegan's Am. and Can. Ch. Chesa's Riverside Imp (left), the all-time top-producing dam of Show Champions, pictured with Ch. Riverside's Song Of The South, and Ch. Riverside's Miss Trial. An outstanding brood bitch is the making of a kennel.

Breeding success: A line-up of six Champions. Pictured left to right: Sh.Ch. Barleyarch Panther, Sh.Ch. Barleyarch Painted Lady, Ch. Isara Kurzhaar Xanthippe, Ch. Barleyarch Platinum, Ch. Isara Kurzhaar Xylophone and Sh.Ch. Barleyarch Polka – all owned by Martin and Sue Harris.

doing it. Breeding really good dogs of any breed is an all-demanding pastime, and the aspirant is frequently bedevilled by quirks of nature. My statement, made originally in *All Purpose Gundog* (Standfast Press, 1976), often quoted and shown to be a simple truth, is that it is perhaps harder to breed good GSPs than some other breeds. "One is not only concerned with handsome dogs, fitting the Standard and being a credit to their breed, but also with producing dogs with inherent characteristics and suitable temperaments potentially fitting them to the task of being good all-purpose gundogs."

AN EXAMPLE OF LINE-BREEDING
To look at an example of considered breeding for quality and type over a long period may be interesting. The pedigree illustrated is that of the a Midlander litter, bred by Mic Layton. The puppies are still babies as these words are written; not yet old enough to prove themselves in any way. But there can be a confident prognosis based on deep experience of their bloodline.

THE 'MIDLANDER TREES' LITTER'S EXTENDED PEDIGREE

DAM'S PEDIGREE

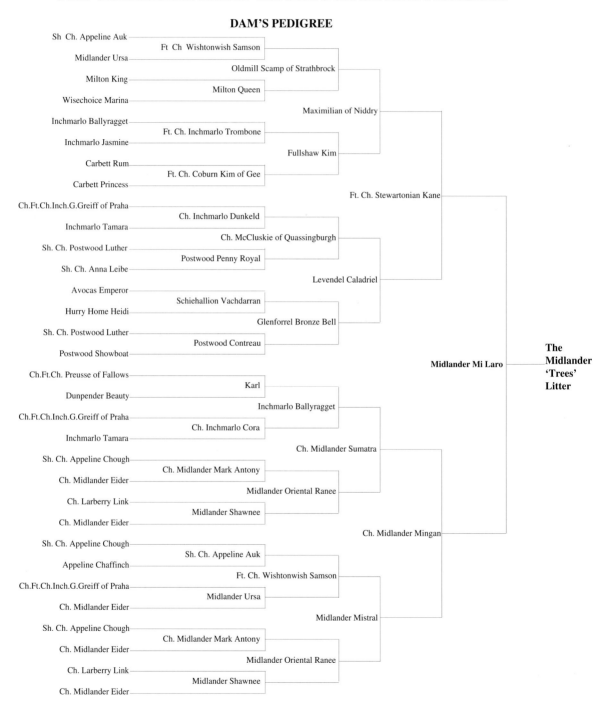

THE 'MIDLANDER TREES' LITTER EXTENDED PEDIGREE

SIRE'S PEDIGREE

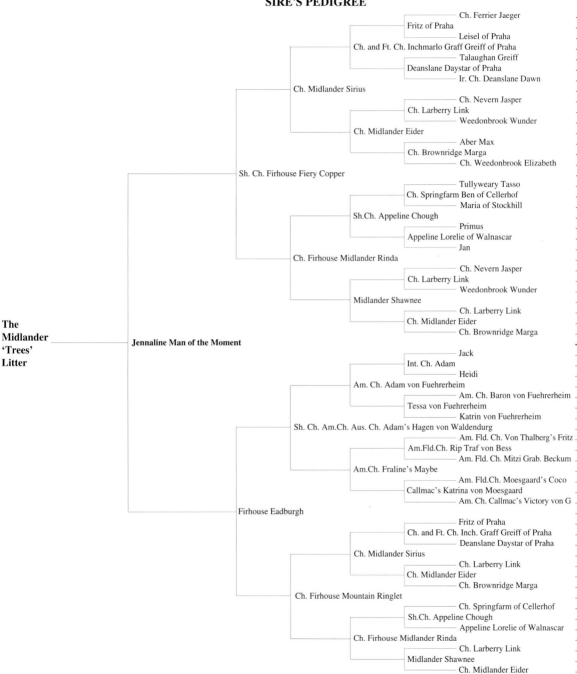

The pedigree, along a single bitch line through thirty-plus years, shows how line-breeding, together with judicious out-crossing, has been used to produce high-quality stock and on-going type. Strangers have been known to come and speak to us, not saying: "That's a GSP, isn't it?" but "That's a Midlander GSP, isn't it?" – and that is the outcome of a third of a century of breeding for good type.

Study the progression. Ch. Brownridge Marga, the foundation bitch of Midlander, was whelped from the post-war import, Ch. Weedondrook Elizabeth, sired by Aber Max, undoubtedly one of the best dogs of his time, though never shown as he was not docked! Marga in due course was mated to Ch. Larberry Link, producing the beautiful and field-talented Ch. Midlander Eider.

Based on the superb quality of Eider and her sire, a father to daughter mating was made; just about as close breeding as one could find. The object was to fix the type; and it did so. Eider successfully produced two litters to Link, and one each to Sh. Ch. Appeline Chough and Ch. and Ft. Ch. Inchmarlo Graff Greiff of Praha. Chough was a good dog carrying excellent blood – his sire was Ch. Springfarm Ben of Cellerhof. Graff Greiff, although another comparative out-cross, was a legend in his own right, being the first UK dog to gain the 'dual' title.

Link and Eider produced Midlander Shawnee. She did not make Champion, but carried all the qualities and temperament Mic was looking for. Later, from Eider and Graff Greiff came a super litter which included Ch. Midlander Sirius, Sh. Ch. Midlander Carina and Midlander Ursa. Ursa, mated to a Chough son, Sh. Ch. Appeline Auk, produced the legendary field worker, Ft. Ch. Wishtonwish Samson. Again from Chough, Eider had whelped Ch. Midlander Mark Antony, and the blood was again strengthened by mating him to Midlander Shawnee, producing Midlander Oriental Ranee. This bitch had it all, and would undoubtedly have made Champion had it not been for the general preference of judges for bigger dogs. She stood 22 inches at the shoulder, but was constantly rejected (regrettably, according to many judges) for not being big enough. If being exactly in the middle of the called-for size bracket is not big enough, one wonders what we are striving for. All 'water under the bridge' now, of course.

Ranee was a good brood bitch and produced Midlander Mistral, sired by Ft. Ch. Wishtonwish Samson, and later Ch. Midlander Sumatra, sired by another very good Field Trial winner and real gentleman, Inchmarlo Ballyragget. Eventually these two Midlanders – Sumatra and Mistral – were mated together and produced Ch. Midlander Mingan; and it was time once more to look for an out-cross.

Ft. Ch. Stewartonian Kane filled the bill perfectly. In three generations he went back to Ft. Ch. Wishtonwish Samson, and in four to Inchmarlo Ballyragget, so he was not a complete out-cross, though nearly so. He was a somewhat rangy, though attractive, dog of terrific temperament and had, after all, won the Kennel Club's prestigious Championship Stake. To be honest, his blood was not very strong in any quarter, and so his prepotency was doubtful. He would have been very much 'a lucky dip' mated to any bitch without strong blood; but to Mingan he looked ideal, and indeed, proved to be so.

The result was near perfection of temperament and type in the production of Midlander Mi Laro. Not yet a Champion in field or show, she is barely three years old. She has shown so much promise and has several Field Trial wins and a Reserve Challenge Certificate under her belt already. I truly believe she is the best GSP I have ever handled in the field; and that is saying something, as there have been many good ones over the years.

Choosing a mate for her was difficult. It was not desirable to further dilute her Midlander blood by another out-cross, but fortunately there was just one dog to fill the role ideally. Jennaline Man Of The Moment was that dog. Sound, successful in the show ring, and a complete gentleman, he already had several Field Trial wins and other awards to his credit. His blood was the perfect 'on paper' match. As can be seen in the pedigree, Man Of The Moment, called Gunther, had double Firhouse parentage, which blood was closely line-bred from Midlander.

So this extended pedigree, through seven generations, is Midlander personified! The litter, the result of half a lifetime of trying to breed good German Shorthaired Pointers, is still in the nest; happy, healthy, and full of promise. Only time will tell!

MATING

The breeder, having decided to mate a bitch and having chosen a sire, should follow a well-trodden path, partly of etiquette and partly of proven worth. It is necessary, of course, to ensure that the sire and dam elect are both registered with the Kennel Club. Having made the decisions, the breeder must now wait until the correct time before carrying out the plan. Bitches normally have seasons, or come on heat, every six months. In some cases the time lapse between seasons may be longer or shorter.

The signs of heat are a swelling of the vulva, the external female sex organ, together with a loss of blood. If a season is suspected, wiping first thing in the morning with a white tissue will show the situation. If there is no blood trace, the bitch is not in season, though she may be by the next day. From the first show of blood, bitches are normally ready for the sire after the ninth day but before the fifteenth. They are usually most willing about the twelfth or thirteenth day. The blood drips clarify commonly by the approach of the third week. This coincides with ovulation, which means that the ova are ready for insemination.

Rarely, bitches may accept dogs at variance with this pattern, but it is unusual. Continuance of the blood flow after twenty-one days is indicative of some problem and a vet should be consulted. It is the complete responsibility of the owner of the bitch to present it to the sire at the right time.

THE MATING AGREEMENT

The prospective breeder should, at an early date, make contact with the owners of the sire and, with their approval, arrange the mating. This is important. No owner of a sire is obliged to accept a mating, and he may not agree to the use of his dog on your bitch. Further, the top stud dogs are in frequent demand and the owners may not want to over-use their dog. Money is not the only consideration. Nevertheless, it is important that the stud fee is agreed beforehand: it is normally payable when the mating takes place.

Bitches are sometimes mated twice, for good measure, about forty-eight hours apart. The fee covers both matings. Quite often, however, the dog, having mated a bitch once will not be interested to repeat the performance the next day. In that case, you can normally be as confident as the sire that the job has been done properly! It is common custom that if a bitch does not conceive, having been apparently properly mated by a proven sire, a free service is offered at the next season. However, it is again important to make sure of this in negotiating with the owners of the sire. Naturally if the sire and dam are both owned by the same person, none of the foregoing is applicable. The bitch always goes to the sire for mating. Owners of sires cannot be expected to be continually travelling the country with their dogs! Having made the arrangements, confirm the situation a few days before going to the sire, and make sure your bitch is in good health, and is not infested with worms. Have a vet check the condition of the bitch, with time in hand to rectify any problem. The responsibility for effecting the actual mating is that of the owners of the stud dog. Leave them to organise and carry out the mating; they know the possible quirks of their dog: If you are asked to assist, follow the instructions given.

PRE-NATAL CARE

Once the bitch has been mated, there is nothing more for the owner to do for several weeks, other than to let the bitch lead a normal life and get plenty of exercise. As the weeks progress through the sixty-three days to the expected birth, the protein value of the bitch's food should be increased and a proprietary brand of multi-vitamins which includes calcium with vitamin D given in the advised dosage. The first signs of pregnancy are likely to be seen in elongation of the nipples, loss of bottom line and perhaps increased appetite. Only high-quality food should be given. It is not desirable for the bitch to get fat.

For many years now, we have used a reputable complete food of the ground, cooked and extruded variety. There are four or five top-class international manufacturing companies who market this type of food. Unlike many of the rolled oats, flaked maize, split peas and 'protein pellet' mixtures, some of doubtful origin, the properly cooked complete foods are highly digestible and are made in a variety to suit all types and ages of dogs. They need nothing added to them, as there is no way they can be improved as a normal diet. They do not, contrary to some people's belief, encourage 'bloat' or stomach torsions. We have fed the appropriate food for our dog's age and activity as advised, and we have proved to our own satisfaction that generations of dogs can survive happily and healthily, and become Champions, on these foods.

WHELPING PREPARATIONS

Asuitable box should be provided for the whelping and for the puppies to live in initially. It should be long enough for the bitch to lie fully outstretched, and still leave width room for a litter of whelps to lie without being crushed by the dam. It should be raised off the floor a few inches, with walls about one foot high, and the front wall fully or partly removable to facilitate the heavily-teated bitch getting in or out, but to be replacable later to contain the pups when they begin to move about.

When the pups are about three and a half weeks old they will start to climb out of the box. This is the time to remove the front again to give them free access to a larger exercise area, but returning to the box to feed from the bitch, rest and sleep. If it is intended that the whelping box be used several times, it should be carefully made of wood and well varnished. This enables it to be washed very satisfactorily and prevents the wood being porous.The top edge should be protected with metal banding angle, otherwise it will almost certainly be damaged by marauders with sharp little teeth! It is essential during the whelping, and for several weeks afterwards, that the box is kept in a draught-free and warm environment. We always use a 300 watt infra-red pig lamp to ensure this. It is made to hang above one end of the box, out of reach of bitch or puppies, who can then choose for their own comfort the warmer or cooler end of the box in which to lie. The hottest area should be about 25 C (80 degrees F). Happy and warm puppies invariably lie out full-stretched and spread around, but cold and unhappy ones huddle together in a pyramid.

It is advisable to introduce the bitch to her box some time well before the expected birth in order that she accepts it as 'home'. Given half a chance the average bitch is quite likely to choose to have her pups in the sitting room or on your bed!

WHELPING

The bitch labours in two distinct periods. The initial labour lasts about twenty-four hours, but is not always noticed by the owners. During this period the whelps move down towards the vulva and other unseen physical changes take place. The onset of the second and productive labour can be easily checked. Almost certainly, the bitch will suddenly refuse food, having previously been ravenous. She will also show a marked drop in body temperature, which is said to prepare the pups for a cooler environment than the inside of the bitch.

Check the temperature of the bitch by carefully inserting a suitable thermometer an inch or so inside the bitch's rectum for a couple of minutes. A drop in temperature from the normal 38.5 to 37 degrees C (101.4 to 99 degrees F) will indicate impending birth. While the normal gestation period is nine weeks, bitches often whelp a few days on either side of this. Only if the whelps are over a week early is there much risk of their non-survival; but if there are no signs of labour after sixty-four days it is advisable to consult your vet.

PHANTOM (FALSE) PREGNANCY

Phantom pregnancies, when everything looks good but no pups result, are not uncommon. Right up to the due time for whelping, the bitch behaves normally and she looks pregnant. She may have swollen teats and milk, but at the last minute all subsides and there are no puppies. All the preparations for impending motherhood are in vain.

Failure to produce puppies can also be due to several other causes. The bitch may have failed to conceive, either because the mating did not coincide with her ovulation, or because there was some reason for her to abort the whelps, maybe unknown to her owners. It is also possible for partly formed whelps to die in the womb and to be reabsorbed by the bitch. If the bitch seems unwell during pregnancy, or there is a dark coloured discharge from her vulva, veterinary advice should be sought immediately.

WHELPING EQUIPMENT

The provision beforehand of several essentials will save panic at the time of the birth. Large quantities of newspapers are excellent for soaking up the mess from the birth, and they are easy to incinerate afterwards. They are also invaluable in keeping the bed dry as the puppies grow older. It is ideal to have several layers of paper in the box, covered by a layer of synthetic lambskin-like blanket which does not absorb the wet, but allows it to filter through to the paper, and is at the same time easily washable. At least 'one to wash and one to wear and one to air' will be required. Straw is certainly not suitable as a bedding for valuable young puppies. It is not sufficiently hygienic. You will also need towels, scissors, warm water and disinfectant; and kitchen scales if you wish to record the birth weights. We also prepare outline whelp shapes drawn on a paper which can be filled in with the coat pattern if the whelps are not solid liver. This helps with early identification and enables us to put all the details of order of birth, time, weight, even a nickname, on one sheet of paper. I suppose some people might even use a camera to record the birth providing it does not upset the bitch, though we have never done so.

ATTENDANCE AT THE BIRTH

Our experience (through some twenty-seven litters of GSPs in thirty-odd years), is that if bitches consider themselves to be part of the family, as all ours have done, they do not object to that family being present at the birth – even in their way demanding it! I think it is only if bitches are strictly kennel dogs that they are likely to wish to be alone to produce their puppies. That does not mean that it is a time to invite the neighbours round. Only one or two people should attend and, if necessary, help at the whelping.

THE BIRTH PROCESS

Early contractions are not always an obvious announcement of impending birth. Sometimes they are ignored by the bitch and not noticed by the owners, and the first evidence is the arrival of a puppy in a rush of water! Most often, however, the bitch becomes restless, scratches at her bedding, cannot find a comfortable position in which to lie, and whines on and off. In such cases, the water is often the first herald of the fact that the birth sac is broken, and the bitch often inspects her rear parts to see if the pup is appearing, which it usually does after a further few contractions.

The puppy will be inside a bag and has to be released from it before it can breathe freely. If the bitch does not do this herself, it is necessary for the attendant owner to break it at least from round the puppy's mouth to allow it to breathe. The whelp is also attached by the umbilical cord to the placenta, or 'afterbirth', which also has to come away from the bitch. It has been attached to the wall of the womb and is the 'food processor' through which the developing whelp was nurtured. The bitch will usually bite through the umbilical cord and will quickly eat the placenta. This is a natural action, possibly induced by nature to keep the bed clean, and is said by some to be an aid to milk production.

If the bitch does none of this, the umbilical cord should be pressed flat between finger and thumb before being cut through at the flattened point, about three inches from the puppy end. The placenta, if present, can then be disposed of. The bitch will usually lick the whelp dry, which also massages it into life, and it will, miraculously, go straight for a teat and start feeding. Again, if this does not occur, it is up to the owner to rub the pup carefully with a dry towel until it cries to signify it is breathing, and after encouraging the bitch to lick it, place it to a teat.

It is advisable to have a separate, smaller box inside the whelping box to place the pups in, maybe with a hot-water bottle well wrapped in blanket at the bottom of it. This will ensure that the bitch does not damage the early arrivals during her scratching around when the subsequent puppies arrive, but can see that the newborn pups are content and near to her. By the time two, three, or four pups have arrived, the bitch will have almost certainly quietened down, and she will happily feed, lick and clean her babies, apparently waiting unconcernedly for the rest of the litter.

Sometimes puppies are breeched, i.e. they come out tail-first rather than head-first. They do not come out as easily this way round, and they breathe a little less readily when first born. Later puppies usually come easier than the first ones, but if excessive contractions over a prolonged period do not produce anything, the vet's advice should be sought. You should also seek expert advice if the bitch tires to the point that all contractions cease over a long period, but she obviously still has puppies as yet unborn. Do not, however, confuse a natural progression of rest periods between whelping with problems. The presence of rather a lot of blood and gore is not unusual, and the bitch may lose blood and a reddish mucus discharge for some time. Only if this continues unnaturally and turns to green or black, should you read danger signals. A bitch producing a big litter of ten or more may well take twenty-four, or even thirty-six hours over it. Look for the danger signals of a distraught and restless, but exhausted bitch, together with cessation of the puppy-producing process while there are more to come – that is the time to seek professional help.

CAESARIAN BIRTH
In the case of major problems, the vet may have to resort to birth by caesarian resection. In other words, he will operate to produce the litter by opening up the bitch and removing the whelps manually from the womb. It is usually quite successful. Bitches recover remarkably well from this major surgery, and the whelps do not seem to suffer at all.

POST WHELPING
We always like our vet to come out and see the bitch within a few hours of the completion of the

A GSP litter at forty-eight hours old. Note how white they are, and the tails are not yet docked.

The same litter two-and-a-half weeks of age: the ticking is now beginning to show.

whelping, in any event. The vet can ensure that all the whelps and the afterbirths have come away, and can also give an antibiotic which will allay any infection. If there are any puppies with malformations which make them unrearable, the vet can deal with them. It is important that your vet is aware of the expected whelping and is prepared to help if necessary.

Whelps should not be handled more than necessary, nor should the bitch be disturbed. She may well wish to go out to relieve herself, but she will be anxious to rush back to her pups as quickly as possible. The bitch will not want to feed, as such, during the whelping, but she may well welcome a small quantity of honey, glucose and warm water or milk, and maybe even a small quantity of beef tea. Her appetite will soon recover and she will need more high protein, easily digested, food to enable her to feed the litter without stress to herself. Bitch and puppies must be kept warm at around 25 degrees C. Chilling is a major factor accounting for the death of many young puppies, and a continual heat source is more important than food in the short term.

ECLAMPSIA

From the time of whelping until the puppies are several weeks old, there is a tremendous requirement for the bitch to produce sufficient milk for her litter. This can result, particularly if the stress is heightened by there being a large number of puppies, in the onset of a condition known as eclampsia, or milk fever.

The first symptoms are that the milk supply dries up, and the bitch shivers and shows signs of unsteadiness. If not treated quickly, the problem can develop to a state of unconsciousness, followed by death in a few hours. However, prompt treatment is usually immediately effective. This consists of the intravenous injection of a heavy dosage of calcium which, of course, must be administered by the vet. Unfortunately, the condition cannot be prevented by giving extra-large quantities of calcium during pregnancy.

Two facts are apparent. The first is that the owner must ensure that the bitch has no more than a reasonable number of whelps to rear. German Shorthaired Pointers do tend to have big litters, but you might consider six or eight whelps to be ideal; ten or twelve to be stressful, and over twelve to be more than reasonable. Reduction of the stress imposed on the bitch can be achieved by hand-rearing part of the litter (not to be recommended) or by culling.

It should be recognised, secondly, that large litters are not the only reason for the condition arising, and the owner should be ever-watchful for the signs – a good reason for the bitch not being left unattended for a protracted period.

DOCKING AND DEWCLAW REMOVAL

Provided the bitch and her litter appear to be content and the bitch has an adequate supply of milk, there is little more to do than arrange with the vet for the tails to be docked. This should be done between two and four days after birth – the bitch being taken out for a walk while it is done, but being returned to the pups as soon as possible afterwards. We have never experienced a problem with docking. Our vet does not stitch, but applies a silver nitrate pencil to the wound immediately, and we never have more than the odd squeak and no bleeding.

It is very important not to dock the tails too short. Your GSP puppies are not to be mistaken by the vet for Boxers or Dobermanns, and the tail left on should be nearer one half of its original length than a quarter. The bitch will look them over and give them a lick when she is returned to the whelping box, but will show no further concern.

Dewclaws are similarly treated at the same time, and although they are easily removed, they cause more concern at the time than the docking.

FEEDING

Apart from ensuring that the bitch has an adequate quantity of good food, you also need to think about weaning the puppies. This used to be a big problem, entailing a lot of work preparing food for the little ones. However, modern science has come to our aid, and the same dog food manufacturers who market the complete foods for adult dogs now market absolutely excellent high-protein, well-balanced and easily digested complete puppy foods. It is in fact possible to start the weaning process with any one of these foods (choose one, and stick with it throughout) at twelve to fourteen days of age. The manufacturers offer a complete advisory service and full instructions for the use of their product. We have reared several litters using one food made by a UK company, and there are several imported brands from the USA and France. There is a certain antipathy towards these prepared complete foods on the part of some older breeders, who still feed their dogs in the old ways. The only advice offered is to do as the manufacturers advise. It is not beneficial to puppies to 'improve' the food by adding meat, milk or whatever. The food contains everything the puppy needs to grow into a happy and healthy dog. One advantage is that by using one of these complete foods, the amateur enthusiast does not give too much of one thing, which can be detrimental to a dog's health, growth and future wellbeing!

WEANING

Another advantage of the commercially produced puppy foods is that the weaning process, from bitch's milk, to puppy food, to adult food, is simplified. Because the puppy food is so satisfying, there is less demand on the bitch to produce milk and by five weeks or so you will find that the puppies do not need her milk at all. The easiest way to dry up a bitch, however, is to ensure that she stands (by this time she is unlikely to lie down) for the litter to take what milk she may still have at least once every day, preferably in the evening.

Again, the manufacturer's instructions for the weaning process should be adhered to, and strong, healthy, well-rounded but not fat puppies will result. Adulteration of the food by the addition of meat or milk to 'improve' it, is almost certain to invite troubles, and we cannot advise too strongly against this. Puppies, or even adult dogs, do not need constant changes of diet for their pleasure or good. Dogs do not have sophisticated tastes like human beings. Indeed, they find food acceptable by smell rather than taste, and will eat the same food, day after day, without being bored by it, providing it satisfies their instinctive needs.

HUMANISING AND SOCIAL INFLUENCES

Puppies deprived of human contact revert to their ancient instinct of being pack animals. Even by eight weeks of age they can have developed an attachment to their littermates and dam to the exclusion of human beings. This trait is rarely reversed, and unbiddable adult dogs can be the outcome. Recognising this factor makes the 'humanising' of puppies imperative. Up to nearly three weeks of age, the puppy brain is not sufficiently developed to be discriminating and the memory is poor. That is why you can cut a tail off and the pup does not remember or hold that against you, providing it is done at three or four days!

However, from three to eight weeks the puppy is receptive to outside influences, so a puppy which is not happy about human beings by eight weeks has great difficulty in adjusting in the forthcoming months. Many people do not realise this. They think that, providing their newly purchased puppy has been fed and watered, the pup will be a normal member of society without question. Not so! Puppies need to get to know and accept humans as the important and good part of their lives, right from the start of their consciousness. If they bond to humans rather than to their littermates, they will keep that feeling all their lives.

This state of affairs is happily achieved by taking every opportunity after the pups are three weeks old to caress and play with them; make them aware that humans are the source of their food and security, until they think they are part of the human family and give their pack allegiance to humans rather than to dogs. We have proved this time and time again, once having experienced a puppy deprived of humanisation and all the heartache that entailed.

At four-and-a-half weeks the litter is now eating solid food, and the puppies are becoming increasingly independent. Note the ticking is now well-developed.

EXERCISE
As the weeks go by, your puppies will become more and more active and will enjoy play periods with you and with their dam. They should have the chance to play outside in the fresh air, providing the weather allows. Pups should not be left to be wet or cold for any prolonged periods, and they should always have access to the safe haven of their warm bed area.

THE 'PICK OF THE LITTER'
Almost all breeders will wish to 'grade' the litter at some time to decide which are the better specimens. Perhaps remarkably, when the whelps are still wet, just out of the dam, the configuration of bones, and the relationship in size of one bone to another, can clearly be seen. For

instance, the relationship in length of the upper and lower arm bones will be the same at birth as the day the dog dies. This is not true of the skull: it develops disproportionately to the rest of the body, and only experience can tell how a head is going to develop.

We believe the best time to assess puppies is when they are five weeks old. At four weeks they are little puddings; at six they have suddenly started to spring on the leg; but at five weeks they most closely resemble the 'balance' which they will display as adults.

SELLING PUPPIES
Never sell a puppy to a person just because the money is put on the table. You owe more to the dogs you are responsible for breeding than that. German Shorthairs are not the ideal dog for everyone, and it incumbent upon the breeder to ensure, as far as is humanly possible, that puppies go to homes where they have every chance to lead a happy and rewarding life.

It is questionable, however, whether a breeder should be responsible for, and take back, any and every one of the puppies that is proffered for return, regardless of the circumstances. When a dog has been treated wrongly for six months or more, it is unlikely ever to be rehabilitated. People buying dogs have as much responsibility as the vendors, and they should not be encouraged to return the unwanted plaything, now severely tarnished, to the breeder. If it were not made so easy, all the 'rescue' organisations would not be overwhelmed with unwanted dogs. By their very existence, they are self-perpetuating – encouraging people to take the easy option, rather than to accept responsibility for what is theirs.

Having said that, it is recognised that in some cases the rescue societies should help, and breeders should not ignore the cries of puppies in adverse conditions through no fault of their own. We always feel that, as responsible breeders, we should be accountable for our family, of which the dogs are a part. We do not consider that we have the right to abnegate responsibility for that for which we have taken possession, certainly not by pushing it off on to someone else's shoulders. The answer is a two-fold maxim: let the buyer and the seller beware.

AFTER-CARE OF THE BITCH
Sometimes it is easy to be so involved with looking after the litter, that the state of the bitch is overlooked. It should be remembered that she has just undergone a gruelling, if natural, experience, and as nature intended, she has given her all to the puppies. She deserves respect, and will almost certainly benefit from some extra care and attention. Her teats may get sore and will be soothed by a healing balm. Her general condition will need rebuilding with the best of food, grooming and open-air exercise – not to mention an extra demonstration of affection!

POSTSCRIPT
Breeding good-quality German Shorthaired Pointers which can grow into fine dogs and go to homes where they are truly appreciated, is a rewarding occupation: but production of a litter of puppies is not a venture to be entered into lightly.

There is a lot of expense; even more work than you might imagine; and, of course, there is always the attendant risk of something going wrong which may result in the death of the bitch. Before mating a bitch, you should ensure that you will be able to find suitable homes for the puppies. You need firm orders; an advertisement in the local paper is unlikely to sell German Shorthaired Pointers – not, at least, to the right people. There is no happiness in owning a fast-growing litter of three or four months with no buyers, as many breeders have discovered to their cost.

It takes hard work on the part of the mother and the breeder to rear a litter of puppies successfully.

Be sure you have considered the issue carefully before breeding, and do not use the excuse that 'it will be good for the bitch and entertaining for the children' – that old wives' tale that was discredited years ago! For the sake of the breed, if you do it, then do it as well as is humanly possible.

Chapter Five

BASIC PUPPY TRAINING

So you have your GSP, and naturally you want to end up with a well-trained dog – one which fits happily into the social scene and the household, and will also be a credit to you in the field, whether in competition or not. It makes no difference whether you have acquired a dog or a bitch puppy, except that a bitch will perhaps be more gentle and loving, against the dog being slightly bolder and more demonstrably affectionate. Dogs do have more masculine drive; but do not confuse that with desire to work – bitches are the equal of dogs in that. My experience is that a bitch desirous to work will be just as brave and bold in the field as her male counterpart, although she may require gentler handling.

INITIAL TRAINING
For the sake of this training programme, let us assume you have a dog puppy, and we will call him 'Solo' – on the assumption you only have one! We should start with the basic requirements of behavioural training for any puppy, whether he is going to work or not. These simple lessons, properly taught, make the difference between an unruly dog and one which is a pleasure to own. Remember that the eight-week-old you have purchased is just a bundle of healthy energy, with no training and no inhibitions, but hopefully already with a firm love of human beings! He has not only to learn his place in the family 'pack', but also to recognise love and affection in addition to discipline; and you have to establish between you a mutual respect. If you do not love and respect your puppy, you cannot expect him to reciprocate.

Training a puppy, whether to live as a family companion dog, or in hopes of eventually owning a Field Trial Champion, requires the same simple approach. All dogs have some inherited traits. GSPs are generally born with an equable temperament and a desire to please. Your puppy will have the instinct to use the wind to find game, to point and to retrieve, but this develops with time, and so eight-week-old Solo will not show any of these facets to his character. It will be many months before he comes to do it all and you can help him to recognise his talents. He does not inherit any instinct to walk to heel or to sit when told, or to be steady to flush, shot or fall of game. He does not instinctively know that you do not want him to chase rabbits. He will find out about his inborn talents in due course, but he will have to learn the pattern of behaviour which will make him an acceptable and useful dog.

The first thing to let Solo learn, by demonstration, is that you are his loving master: that you represent safety, fun, food, happiness and security. Having a dog which does things for you because he loves you, recognises you as his pack leader and wants to please you, is the situation to be aimed for. If you live in a family group it is essential that your puppy gets to know and accept

Most GSP puppies have an equable temperament and a desire to please.

all its members. Equally, they must understand that they have some responsibility towards the happiness and contentment of the puppy. However, you must be the dog's trainer; and while your children, if old enough to behave sensibly, may enjoy Solo's play periods, and you may all go out walking together, you must establish yourself as the pack leader and only you must carry out the training programme. Solo will be confused if he suddenly finds he has three or four masters, each with a possibly different approach.

However, do not shut your family out from the puppy either; there will come a time when you will need help with the training, and all should enjoy the new member of the family. There is no happy outcome for you or Solo if he is unwilling, afraid or bullied. Though better equipped than some other breeds, Solo is like all dogs in that he has a tiny brain compared with yours. He has virtually no reasoning power or intellect. He will learn only by experience, though he will be clever enough to remember such experience, particularly if repeated often, and will not forget what he learns.

Having the opportunity to run on the wind, to find out how his nose works for him (and you), is essential for him to learn about his own capability as a game-finder. You cannot teach him that, but you can lead him to the experience. It is a basic truth that you can teach your dog to be obedient, to run backwards and forwards across the wind and to retrieve dummies on command; all this in a public city park. But if you want Solo to know about partridges, how to recognise their scent from 50 yards or more; to know that with care and stealth he can hold them on point until you come up with your gun – this he cannot learn in the park. To learn about game he has to have contact with it; and he will only learn his lessons properly if he is given the chance to get experience, time after time, after time, after time, and so on.

A Pointer cannot become a 'bird dog' by learning lessons of obedience. The dog has to experience the real thing, repeatedly. Everything your dog learns is from repeated experience, eventually from understanding what you require, until it is etched deeply into the memory. None of this should put you off, however. It is not difficult to train a GSP to great heights of performance, providing the groundwork is done thoroughly and correctly.

PRE-SCHOOL LEARNING

You can start playing learning games with a very young puppy, just as you might with a toddler in the family. For instance, Solo will sleep a great deal, but the moment he wakes up he will want to urinate. So be aware of this and, as soon as he wakes, pop him outside into an enclosed, safe place and encourage him to perform. Praise him when he does so and let him come in again. Your puppy will most frequently want to relieve himself when he awakes and after eating. Be sure you get into the habit of giving him the chance to do so outside, before he gets into the habit of doing it on the carpet. You can be sure that, one way or the other, he will learn by experience and make a habit of what he learns.

As soon as Solo comes to recognise the smell, sight and sound of his food preparation, you can be pretty sure he will come towards it. This is the time to teach him to come to call, using the same words and the same encouraging tone every time, perhaps his name and the command – "Solo, come". It really does not matter what words you use, providing they are short and clear, and the same every time.

But when Solo is preoccupied with some distraction, do not expect, in early days, a response to a recall command. In fact, if you wait until he is chasing the neighbour's cat across the lawn before you call him, it is almost certain that he will not obey you. What is worse, you will actually have taken a step towards teaching to ignore your command: the exact opposite of what you intended. Only call your puppy to come towards you when he is actually already doing so. Then he will learn to associate the command with the action; and after twenty or thirty such experiences Solo will begin to learn the meaning of the command, and if he loves and respects you, he will obey it! When the habit is strong enough, he will obey the command at all times, regardless of other distractions.

COMMAND TO SIT

If you want to teach your puppy to sit down, do not say, "Solo, sit, sit, sit" repeatedly. You will only become frustrated and your puppy will be bewildered. He probably does not understand what you want or does not realise that the command is imperative. Be near to your puppy, attract attention by saying his name and command "Solo, sit" in a firm but not aggressive voice. Hold your puppy, probably on a lead at first and with one hand push down gently but firmly on his back end. As he sits, repeat the command once. Do this twenty times and he will learn – from experience – that the command "Sit" means just that.

Try always to ensure that whatever you ask of your puppy is clear and simple, show him by example what you want him to do (though he will not learn the command "Sit" by watching you do it!). Praise when he gets it right, but do not be too hard if Solo fails because he did not understand. Make all the lessons fun for him and they will be fun for you too. Keep the lessons short but repeat them frequently. Five minutes, two or three times every day, will achieve far more than two hours every Saturday morning.

INTRODUCTION TO A LEAD

There is some argument regarding the permanent use of a collar for dogs, though if you live in a place where the dog can get out into a public place (do not *ever* let that happen if you can avoid it), your puppy must by law be wearing an identification tag, which probably means wearing a collar. For normal training, a simple nylon woven strap lead with a slip loop at one end and a hand loop at the other is ideal. It is worn always with the lead loop starting by the dog's right ear and going under and round the neck through the link ring, and up to your hand. This is assuming the dog is going to walk on your left side which is normal; you carry your gun under your right arm. If the

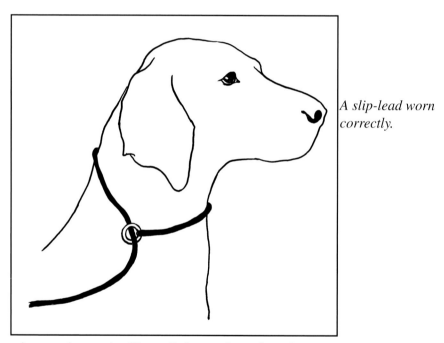

A slip-lead worn correctly.

lead runs the opposite way it will not slip loose when released.

Teaching Solo to accept a lead is easy. Just put it on and let him go where he will as much as possible, and only ease him into accepting the restriction of it. Solo will soon become accustomed to it and will not object until he tries to pull away from you. Encourage Solo gently to come with you as you walk, keeping him to your left with the lead crossing in front of your body and held in your right hand. Your left hand is free to hold the lead but is not doing so. Again, as always, prefix the command with the dog's name and say "Solo, heel". Give a short sharp tug on the lead with your left hand and immediately release it again. The lead tightens momentarily round Solo's neck, pulling him back, but within a split second is loose again and he has no discomfort.

Talk encouragingly to your dog as you walk, and while the lead is loose be satisfied that he is coming with you. Only if he moves forward so that the lead is taut again do you repeat the process of tugging the lead and repeating the command. Praise him for getting it right. If the action is done so that any effect on the puppy is only of a fraction of a second duration, the dog will quickly learn to walk to heel without pulling. If you merely use the lead as a restrictive rope, Solo or any other dog will soon learn to accept it as an unpleasant fact of life and will pull all the time he is on the lead. Perfection is not achieved in minutes, of course; the lesson must be repeated time and time again; always with the same words, always with the same action and always with praise for compliance. In due course, Solo will react to the command "Heel", whether on the lead or not. Get your puppy accustomed to having the lead taken off and replaced without Solo moving. It is very easy to always let the puppy run free as soon as he is off the lead and he will see its removal as the signal to go. As with all commands, do not let the puppy learn by practice what the next command will be. Introduce variations and Solo will accept that he cannot anticipate the next command.

COMMAND TO STAY

A similar progression is undertaken to teach the puppy to stay. Sit the puppy, by command, on the lead. Give the command "Solo, stay", holding the lead in your right hand and with your left hand raised, palm open, facing towards the puppy (this is a hand signal which will be used later in field work). Slowly move back to the extent of the lead. Counter any attempt to move by quickly repeating the command and, if necessary, moving back to the puppy to replace him in position. You will be surprised how quickly Solo learns to wait until you return and praise.

Next you can lie the lead carefully on the floor and repeat the lesson, gradually extending the time and the distance you move away. In a short while you will be able to stay away from your puppy for a minute or more without him moving. Never, in early training call your puppy to come to you from the sit and stay position. Always go back to your puppy. He will learn never to move until you come back. Expand the lesson as he learns: walk round him; move away and come back but continue past, keeping Solo in the Stay position. Commonsense will tell you when to extend the time and distance, but the maxim is always to progress slowly, ensuring that the puppy understands before you expect him to learn the lesson and be one hundred per cent obedient to the command.

GIVING PRAISE

All the simple obediences required of a companion dog are taught in the same manner. Make the lessons clear and short, and the younger the dog, the less pressure you must put on him to obey. Praise for something done well is essential, but do not be over-lavish. A quiet pat and a "good dog" is sufficient. Do not encourage uncontrollable excitement after any lesson. You can praise good work by the reward of a tidbit, but take care not to let this become a habit. If you do so, the puppy will come to look for the tidbit as an essential reward and will not otherwise obey.

As you progress with lessons you will find that the puppy pays increasingly respectful attention to you, sometimes even apparently anticipating your wishes. You can establish a lovely rapport with your puppy quite early in life, and you will enjoy the lessons together. This rapport will grow, and once established between you will last all of your dog's life, and you will both be happy in the other's company.

PROBLEMS

It is easy in a book to say, 'Do this, do that and the dog will respond'. It is also true that sometimes the dog may not respond, and the lesson is a failure. If this happens you must go back to simple

As lessons progress, your GSP will pay increasingly respectful attention to you.

beginnings and start again. Providing your GSP puppy has a normal brain and you approach training in such a way that he has confidence in himself and in you, he will learn the lessons. However, it can be just possible that you have been unlucky enough to buy a puppy with impaired mental capacity. Just as with children, it is rare but not impossible, and is not easy to recognise at an early age. It may be that in such a case the dog is not suitable for training. Also it is a fact that not all dogs like all humans or vice versa.

If you really feel, after a few months, that you are not establishing any rapport with your dog, you could seek professional advice. It may be that you are making some basic error, or that the puppy is just not accepting you as an individual. If the latter is the case, you probably do not have any love for the puppy either. Such feelings are usually mutual, and a change of ownership may be indicated. In every locality there is a dog training club where the tutor would be happy to offer advice, and assuredly your GSP puppy will suffer no harm from being a pupil with you at a few classes, particularly if you are a completely novice dog-owner.

OTHER COMMANDS
The basic lessons required to be taught should include the following:

"No" – to cease any unwanted activity.
"Toilet" – when the dog is in a position to obey.
"Come" – to recall your dog.
"Sit".
"Stay".
"Down"– if you want to teach him to lie down.
"Heel".
"Get On" – a releasing command for the dog.

Only a few of these action commands are directly related to field work, but as we will see, they all have some influence in the behaviour of the finally trained gundog.

TO DO OR NOT TO DO
Now you have an idea of some of the activities you should follow to help your puppy grow into a well-balanced dog. Before we go on to further training there are a few 'do not' activities to be avoided at all costs if you want to have a good gundog when your puppy matures.

PUNISHMENT
Do not hit Solo as punishment – it does not achieve the desired result. If you have treated your puppy gently, to chastise by voice will probably be an effective deterrent, but do not shout. Your puppy is not deaf, but can readily develop 'cloth ears' if shouted at continually. The only physical punishment recommended is to shake your puppy firmly by the scruff of the neck – and growl at him – yes, growl at him! That is exactly what his dam did if he displeased her when he was a baby. And because he learned to understand and respect that, he will do so now.

Even so, be sure that the punishment is clearly related to the crime. Your puppy will not understand if you try to punish him for something he did two hours ago. Any chastisement must be immediate and clearly related to the wrong-doing. Do remember that it will be a retrograde step to punish your puppy, even in the mildest way, without being absolutely certain that he knows that he has done wrong wilfully – not just because he did not understand what you asked of him.

GAMES TO AVOID
Do not play 'ball' with your gundog puppy. Let Solo have a ball as a toy by all means, but do not use it for retrieving practice. Similarly, do not use a wooden dumbbell for retrieve training. A dumbell is for Obedience dog training, not for gundogs. It is desirable that everything Solo has in his mouth to retrieve has the basic softness and texture of dead game, which is why a canvas gundog dummy is ideal.

Never play 'tug-of-war' with your puppy. Oh, he will love it, of course, but it will not be good for young developing teeth and, worse still, will teach him that he has the right to challenge you for possession – one thing he does not want to learn.

Whenever you are training your puppy, try to foresee the problems you might encounter in the execution of any particular exercise. For instance, when retrieve training, in the early days, do not stand in the middle of a field: it is almost certain that Solo will run past you and round in circles with the dummy, not wishing to relinquish it. But if you stand just through a gateway, or gap in a hedge, or between buildings, Solo is forced into coming directly to you: and that also will become a habit.

MORE THAN ONE DOG

A brief word of warning before leaving the subject of basic puppy training. Whatever you might think, it is not a good idea to have two puppies, whether from the same litter or not, at the same time. A considerable amount of research has been done which shows that when puppies are together their pack instinct to one another is strengthened, which weakens their tie to the unwary owner. Invariably one puppy proves to be a stronger character than the other. Either the bold one dominates the weaker one and becomes, in his own view, pack leader, and so difficult to train; or the weaker one is so subjugated that he lacks the confidence to achieve his potential. If numbers of dogs are kept, it is advised that they are at least eighteen months apart in age. In any event, do not attempt to train your puppy at the same time as you are exercising other dogs; the distraction is too great and you will only get a satisfactory response if you and the trainee are alone.

Chapter Six

FIELD WORK TRAINING

INTRODUCTION
In order to bring your GSP's training for field work to fruition, it is necessary to understand in the first place what you are attempting to achieve. This is an all-purpose gundog: the GSP has to be a hunting Pointer, working wide sweeps of open ground, hunting on the wind for game scent and pointing staunchly when game is found. The GSP may also have to work like a Spaniel, hunting close through heavy cover and flushing game out for the guns. Your GSP has to be a Retriever. That does not mean running to a shot bird and fetching it back to you. The dog must be steady, to flush, flight, shot and fall. Your GSP must only retrieve on command and must be capable of finding the scent of a wounded, running bird and must be able to follow it to make the retrieve, always carrying the game tenderly, bringing it to hand, and never damaging it: all this from land or water.

In training, the danger is that one succeeds so well in one facet that another becomes a failure. For instance, an over-free and only partly obedient hunter, is likely to be unsteady when it comes to the retrieve; or a perfectly behaved retriever may be inhibited when it comes to using initiative to run and hunt. But GSPs do have the potential to be equally competent at all these aspects of the work schedule. Your dog is very biddable and can be trained to a very high degree of efficiency.

The same rules apply to field training as to basic obedience. Your dog will only learn by understanding and by repetition. Do not think that you can train your dog in a few days, or even a few weeks, or months. It is a slow progression, but having succeeded you will have a good shooting companion for ten years or more.

TRAINING METHODS
There are many methods of training gundogs. However, I am quite sure that the broad principle of training gently but firmly, by repetition, is the basic rule applied the world over, and it is used with variation by every gundog trainer I have met, in all the English-speaking countries of the world. The electric collar, though I believe popular in the USA, is not a training aid I see as essential, nor is the system of 'forced' retrieving. The training method I outline has proved successful for me over thirty-odd years in the training of a great number of gundogs. Many others trainers have followed the method successfully too.

THE SYLLABUS
These are the important factors you should get clear in your mind before embarking on training your GSP (for this purpose, known as 'Solo') to become a competent gundog:

RIGHT: A training session with David Layton: the whistle is an essential item of equipment for the gundog handler.

Nash.

BELOW: The Sit (already taught by voice) is now indicated by one long blast of the whistle and the appropriate hand signal – left hand open, palm forward and arm raised.

Nash.

1. Solo must understand the signal or command given. For this reason it is imperative that the same commands are given every time, without variation of words or tempo. Do not let your enthusiasm, laziness, frustration or ill temper affect the command and make it sound different to your dog. As training develops many commands are given by hand signal and by whistle. These have the advantage that they do not fluctuate with your personal feeling of the moment. It is difficult to express frustration with a whistle command!

2. Solo has accepted that you are the pack leader and is willing – even eager – to obey you.

3. Solo is 'conditioned' into accepting the command, having heard it so many times, and reacted to it in one way; it becomes a habit to do so, and the command will produce the same action this and every time it is given.

None of this pre-supposes intelligence in the accepted human sense. Solo has not reasoned or deduced any facts without experience. He has learned by repetition and has a good memory to retain the experience. Dogs become very clever and very wise. Shorthairs do have incredibly good memories and learn readily, providing the lesson is within the realm of their limited understanding. Never fall into the trap of thinking that your dog can apply reasoned thought, as can a human being. While your GSP has a receptive brain and a good memory, reasoning power is very limited, and mostly the ability to learn is only related to repeated experience.

MORE BASIC OBEDIENCE

Having considered the part of the dog-work which is taught by the handler, now recognise that a great part of Solo's performance relies on inherited instincts; and they must be channelled into an acceptable pattern, for your GSP to be a valued gundog. The fact that Solo must be given the chance to discover inherited capabilities has already been mentioned, but before your dog goes to big running ground it is desirable to have some training in obedience. To obey the whistled "Stop" command is the most important lesson your dog will learn; this is taught hand-in-hand with retrieving (activities in hunting and pointing are separate) so the two must be carried on in parallel. Now is the time to add to the basic things Solo has assimilated, and lessons must be taught relating to:

1. Walking to heel on and off the lead.
2. Sit and Stay to the whistle at distance.
3. Recall from distance.
4. Simple retrieving.
5. Steadiness to shot and fall and distractions.

The most important is the 'Sit and Stay to whistle at distance', which from now on we will call the "Stop" whistle. If you can be sure that this command will be obeyed, regardless of situation or distraction, then you can give Solo free rein to run and hunt across the wind, and never be fearful that he will go out of control. Your dog can be stopped from chasing fur, stopped from running ten fields away. He will not run in to retrieve, or be beyond your control in any circumstance. It is not as difficult as it sounds to achieve this, if you go the right way about it. Secure in the faith that you have control over your dog, you can put him into situations where he can learn to use his inherited instincts to the best advantage.

SIGNALS: VOICE, WHISTLE, HAND

Generally, when working in the field, you will give signals to Solo by hand or whistle, rather than by the spoken word. The signals which you need to teach are as follows:

SIT (already taught by voice): Whistle – one long blast. Hand Signal – Left hand open, palm forward and arm raised.

This becomes the "Stop" command and is the most important signal to teach thoroughly. Progress from a starting point of Solo being within one yard of you, then two yards, then five, ten, fifteen, twenty and so on, until the dog obeys instantly at 100 yards. Never try to jump from five yards to fifty; short-cuts are bound to end in failure. Remember that the easy way for Solo to obey any subsequent command is to get him to stop first. He has then acknowledged that he is paying attention to you and will be receptive to further instructions.

CHANGE DIRECTION WHILE HUNTING: Whistle – one short pip to attract attention, (or in early stages, the stop whistle). Hand Signal – a clear wave of the arm in the desired direction.

In practice, you will find that to stop Solo first, gain his attention, and then give the hand signal, is most successful. But as the dog becomes experienced, that signal may even be reduced to a flick of the hand or even a nod of the head. Dogs are very receptive to body language and the rapport between dog and handler can be so close that the dog almost appears to read the handler's mind.

GO LEFT, GO RIGHT: Whistle – again, the short pip to attract attention. Hand Signal – a clear wave of the arm in the desired direction.

This command is most likely to be used when the dog has been sent out to make a blind retrieve and is at some distance, and the handler wishes to put the dog in a specific area to seek the game.

COME (the recall): Whistle – two or three consecutive short blasts. Hand Signal – pat the left thigh with the left hand. It has to be said that a popular alternative hand signal has recently appeared on the British scene. It is to adopt the 'crucifix' position, with both arms out-stretched. This signal must only be for use by people who play at the game but are not shooters. What would you do with your gun? All hand signals should be such that they can be given with one hand, preferably the left one, as most people carry their gun under the right arm. Surely the object of the whole exercise is to have a dog with which you can go shooting

GO BACK: Whistle – long blast first to stop the dog. Hand Signal – hand open, palm forward, and the arm raised and thrust forward as if to push open a door, together with the command "Go Back".

FETCH (to make a retrieve): Word command – "Get on and fetch". Hand Signal – arm thrust forward in the direction of the retrieve, under-arm.

GO BACK AND FETCH: Word command when your dog is at distance, to send him further back to make a blind retrieve. Hand Signal – as "Go Back".

FETCH FROM IN OR OVER WATER: Word command – "Get over (or in) and fetch". Hand signal – as "Fetch".

HI LOST: Voice signal only. Often used as "Fetch" but more usefully kept as an indication, when directed to the area of a blind retrieve, that the dog is in the area and should use initiative to find.

LEAVE: Voice signal only. To leave any unwanted activity, such as your dog investigating the

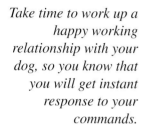

Take time to work up a happy working relationship with your dog, so you know that you will get instant response to your commands.

Nash.

remains of a rotting carcase, but also at the time of fall of game or dummy to commence memory retrieve process.

Be careful to always tell Solo if he is to go out to find and make a retrieve. The word "Fetch" is the important command. It is essential that Solo should understand the difference between going out to hunt and going out to retrieve. I have seen many handlers in severe difficulties because their GSP did not appreciate the difference.

WHISTLES

Commands given by voice do not have to be shouted; dogs normally have good hearing capability. Most handlers use a whistle made of plastic or horn. There is also a 'silent' whistle on the market, which some prefer. Few handlers rely on their own mouth whistle. In some gale-force wind conditions your dog may not be able to hear the normal whistle, so it is advisable to have a loud blast whistle as a back-up. Do not use it except to get the dog accustomed to it or in extreme conditions.

GUN-SHY OR GUN-HAPPY

The question of introduction to gunshot, or even to the gun itself, is something you should always try to make as natural as possible. All through early life, let Solo hear saucepan lids dropped, doors banged and blanks fired at a distance. Let him see you with the gun regularly, and right from day one. Fire your shotgun a few times at least 100 yards from the pup. If this approach is used, it is very unlikely that your puppy will even be gun-nervous, let alone gun-shy.

The first time Solo is given the opportunity to associate the shot with a retrieve, again fire the gun at a distance and aimed away from the dog. It will not take the youngster long to realise that the shot indicates a possible retrieve. Before long Solo will hear the shot and look, not for the gun, but wider out to see and mark the fall. It is said that experienced GSPs out hunting with a very bad shot who continually misses, will give up in disgust and go back to the car! It is certain that once a dog knows that you are going to shoot the game produced from the point, he will show surprise and even regret when you miss!

The one thing you must not do is to introduce Solo to gunshot by firing a 12 bore over the dog's head 'to see if he is gun-shy'. Almost certainly he will be! I believe that gun-shyness is often shown by otherwise very nervous dogs, and this extreme of sensitivity can assuredly be inherited. However, you should look for some sensitivity in a youngster; that type of dog will be sensitive to game scent too. Alternatively, the self-assured, brash dog is not likely to be gun-shy – but may be a difficult dog to train!

If your dog does display gun-nervousness, then this can be overcome by following the above procedures very slowly and carefully. It is not to be confused with gun-shyness, which, to the best of my knowledge, is incurable. *A truly gun-shy dog can never be trained as a gundog.* Though a gun-shy dog could possibly be used for other purposes, innate nervousness may render him less than satisfactory – you would have to consider the individual case.

Chapter Seven

HUNTING

SCENT

A dog who is not a good hunter, is not a good German Shorthair. This is the basic skill which makes a GSP. GSPs hunt with their noses for scent of game, not with the eyes for a view of it. This brings us to the question of what scent is, and how the dog understands it. It is not an easy thing to explain; unfortunately humans have very poor scenting capability and even our best scientists know little enough about how scent is carried.

It is known that game-birds give off scent (or a smell, if you like), though man does not have the delicacy of nose to detect it. That scent is in some way molecular and is carried on the wind: particularly well on a gentle breeze of damp, warm rising air, and fitfully in hard, blowing wind and cold conditions. It is that indication of the presence of game which your GSP seeks. Solo will run with his head at the most efficient height to take the scent as it is in the circumstances, but he will lift his head high to take a distant scent on the wind, and this high head carriage is considered desirable by purists. I, personally, like to think my dog is running with an urgent desire to find scent and knows at any particular moment what head carriage will be most efficient!

It should be understood that it is essentially scent on the air that your dog seeks. Solo should not, and will not, if he knows his job, seek for what is called 'foot' scent, left on the ground by running game, though he will and should seek 'foot' or 'blood' scent on the ground to follow and effect the retrieve of a wounded, running bird.

UNDERSTANDING WIND DIRECTION

Once recognising an air scent of game, Solo is capable, with practical experience, of locating fairly exactly the source of the scent and will freeze to immobility with his nose pointing at the game and body rigidly outstretched. GSPs are born with a natural desire to hunt for this scent. This means that your dog can, and will, run 'across' the wind to find game and will point it when he does so. Running across the wind means running at right-angles to the way it comes to him.

In initial training, Solo must always be given the opportunity to run on this frontal wind, but with experience will learn to use the wind to best advantage, whatever direction you put him down to run and hunt. In other words, you, as the handler, must walk into the wind and your dog must be encouraged to run across your front from left to right and back again. If Solo only ran directly into the wind, the width of the ground he hunted would be no more than a yard or two. But if he runs at an angle across the wind, he has the wind coming equally on one cheek or the other as he runs to the left or the right. Your dog cannot take scent on the wind if it is coming from behind him, and if he takes it head-on he can only take it on a narrow front. But by running at right-angles to the wind

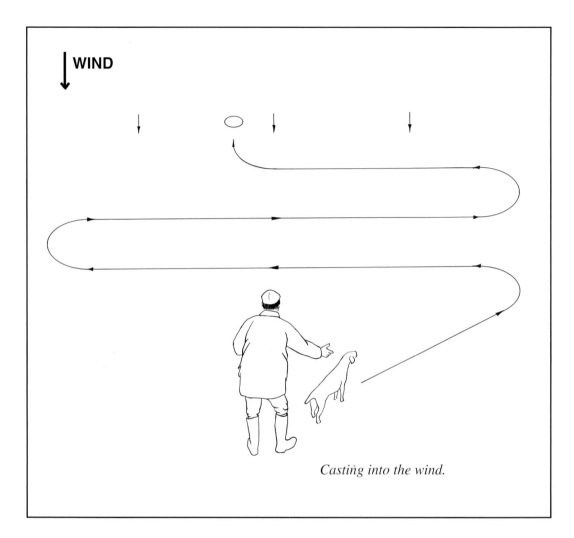

WIND

Casting into the wind.

direction, he can take the scent from the windward side. Thus your dog can quarter (this is what running across the wind is called) on as wide a front as you or the terrain dictate, with opportunity to find game on all the width of the run. It is important for you to understand wind direction to be able to help your dog. Even on a very still day there is always some air movement, and scent will ride on the air, however little movement there is. Remember that you are teaching some other skills in parallel with hunting; and hunting and pointing essentially go together. But for the purpose of clarification they should be studied separately, and we will discuss pointing in more detail later.

Solo must learn to deal with wind from various directions. A particular situation may demand one treatment or another, but the object is always the same, i.e. to let the dog run across the wind rather than directly into it or with it behind him. The width of the quarter depends entirely on circumstances – terrain, growth of crops and visibility. On a moorland covered with heather, the home of the grouse, the dog may work a beat several hundred yards wide. In agricultural land the width may be determined by the size of the fields or by the restriction of hedges or fences. In woodland and close cover, keeping contact with your GSP is important. In the broad sense, there is no value in having Solo on point if you cannot see him. Therefore his beat should be restricted to a width which is reasonable, both for you to see him, and for you to make progress through whatever undergrowth there might be.

For example, if you are in a wood with large patches of rhododendron bushes which are very dense, Solo might have to stay close to the gun (within shooting distance), and to perform like a Spaniel, forcing his way through the cover and flushing the game out rather than pointing it. In such a case, Solo can be discouraged from pointing and kept moving forward with the quiet command "Get on, get on" or similar. Another controlling factor of the width of the beat is that Solo must not only find and point game, but must present it to the gun(s). If there is only one person shooting over the dog, the beat will not be as wide as if there are four guns about thirty or forty yards apart. All is determined by practical considerations.

Again, it is surprising how quickly Solo will learn to adjust to the conditions, and indeed, to the presence of game. An experienced GSP will run hard to search for scent, but will slow the pace and become a much more stealthy animal in the close proximity of game as he comes to the exact location and locks on to point. In clear, open ground Solo should run hard, searching for scent, but in cover where there may be birds but where scent can be difficult to 'read', he should progress more carefully.

QUARTERING

In teaching to quarter, or rather in putting Solo into the situation where he can come to realise what his capability is, do not worry too much about a very wide range initially. If necessary, when Solo reaches the extremity of the desired beat, drop him with the stop whistle, and having gained his attention, give a clear arm signal to change his direction to hunt back across your front. You will find that Solo will soon learn to react to a short pip on the whistle and will look up in anticipation of the signal you are going to give him. The control signals you will use when at a distance are all taught in the basic field and retrieve training sessions and can be studied in the chapters relating to the subject.

THE CHECK CORD

There are occasions when the use of a long check-cord could be of help in training. It will keep an unruly dog within bounds, even if the cord is merely dragging on the ground. Such an aid should only be used in absolutely open ground where it cannot get tied up, but is really unnecessary providing Solo is obedient to the drop whistle. Once having stopped your dog from doing wrong by using the drop whistle successfully, take care in how you cast him off again.

For instance, if you have stopped him just as he was taking off after a hare, be sure not to cast your dog in the direction the hare took, or he may resume the chase. Sometimes, in training days it is even desirable to keep your dog at the drop, just as you did when initially teaching the Sit and Stay, and to walk over to him. It is in this situation that the value of good training to the basic obediences is truly underlined.

WORKING GROUND

Do not think that you must keep to the centre of the ground Solo is quartering. Sometimes, for reasons best known to your dog (probably the strength or direction of a swirling wind), he will quarter much further to one side of you than the other. Adjust your position to allow Solo to work

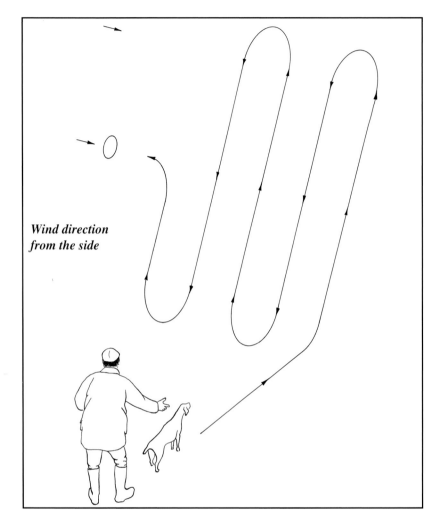

Wind direction from the side

Casting down-side of the wind.

as he wants, providing it is within the parameters of the occasion. If there is a side wind from the right, you will need to cast out to the left and let Solo quarter across the wind but working across from your left to your right. Give a chance and encourage your dog to do this, and do not walk the ground until Solo has had the opportunity to hunt on it. If necessary, go out to the down wind (in this case, left-hand side of the beat) and cast your dog off from there.

Solo will be most efficient as a game-finder if he starts at the 'bottom' of the wind. In fact, the wind will draw him into it, and if he starts halfway across to the right, you will have difficulty in getting him to cover the ground on the down-wind side, to your left. Remember that it is the job of dog and handler in partnership to produce game for the guns (even if you are the only gun!), and your dog will perform most efficiently within the determined boundaries if you start him off at the

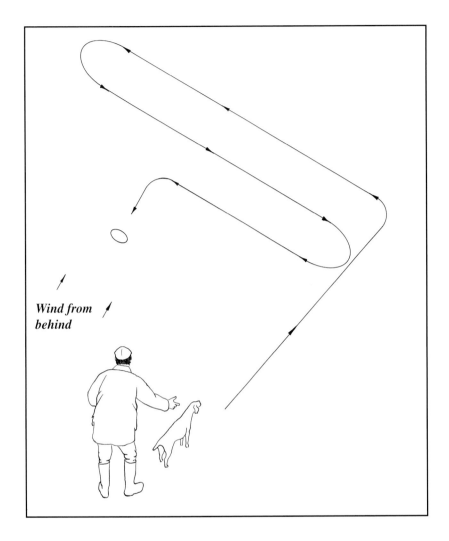

Casting the dog out down the side of the beat to get below the wind and to quarter back towards the handler.

Wind from behind

right place. However, Solo will come to know a great deal more about finding game than you will, and he should not be unnecessarily hampered in that task by over-handling.

DOWN-WIND HUNTING

If you and Solo are forced into the situation, because shooting dictates, where he must hunt for game whilst you are going down-wind, your dog must be cast out down one edge of the beat in order that he can get beyond the potential game and can hunt back up the wind towards you. Solo must be forgiven for failing to point any birds encountered as he goes out down-wind, but should acknowledge (it is called honouring) them going away. You and the guns must stand still and give your dog the opportunity to work the ground in front as he quarters towards you.

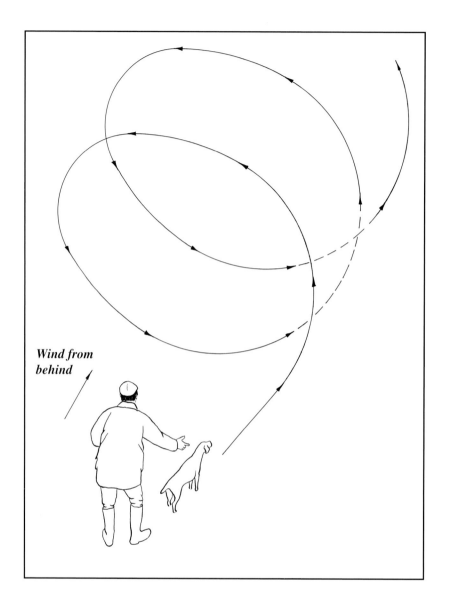

A practical alternative.

Wind from behind

PUTTING IT ALL TOGETHER
Solo will learn from every experience, though some dogs learn faster than others. No doubt some have stronger basic instincts than others, too, but even the slow learner will come to a degree of efficiency eventually if he gets enough experience. Very often the realisation of what hunting is all about comes in a rush to an apparently slow-learning dog. The dog suddenly becomes aware of the object of the exercise, realises the part he has to play, and goes on to be a very competent gundog.

Chapter Eight

POINTING

THE INSTINCT TO POINT

If you have ever seen a cat, poised and ready to pounce on a hapless mouse, you have seen that same primitive instinct which is developed in 'pointing' dogs and which gives them their *raison d'etre*. Your GSP's ancestors were selected for breeding because they showed a natural talent to use their nose to find game, because they had that inborn tendency to freeze in its presence, and were biddable enough for their owners to avert the dog's instinct to catch and eat what they caught. Generation upon generation of Pointers developed slowly through a programme of careful choice based upon performance – always looking for the best, refining that delicate skill to its optimum.

Today your GSP can be relied upon, with suitable training, to find game by scent and to staunchly indicate its position by adopting a rigid stance aimed at defining the quarry's exact location. That is what we call pointing. Not only does the trained pointer do that, holding the point for as long as necessary for guns to get up to it, but also, upon command, flushing the game to present it to the guns. I remember the first time I saw this happen. The time was about 1956, and my wife and I were in the company of a new-found friend, John Gassman, a German who had come to England to escape Nazism twenty years earlier. Sadly he is no longer with us. We were being given, for the first time, a demonstration of what German Pointers can do. I was dumbstruck by the mystery, the beauty and majesty of it all. The whole process, if based on our human conception of scent, was so improbable as to be almost unbelievable. And yet there in front of me, some thirty yards ahead, was this rigidly posed dog. Only a moment before he had been running hard to find scent; but suddenly he had slowed, his movements became lynx-like: carefully, oh so carefully, he edged forward, came to within a few yards of I knew not what, and froze.

We came up beside the dog, and John commanded him to flush. In he went, quite under control and up came a covey of partridges from where they had crouched, completely hidden in the moderately long grass. We did not shoot, indeed we had no gun, and the dog sat and watched the birds away. I had no idea that the birds were there until the dog pointed them. At that moment I knew I had to have a pointing dog. It is strange, in a way, that until that day I had spent a lifetime with dogs in variety, but had not thought of owning a pointer. It was the perfect example of love at first sight; and after nearly forty years I am still entranced by this enigmatic and mysterious capability which sets Pointers and Setters apart from all other breeds of dogs.

THE EARLY EXPERIENCES

So this is the characteristic capability of the pointing breeds: the desire and ability to run and hunt

Brian and Jean Botterman's Ft.Ch. Montabber Corriefeuran

Cecilia Weller's Am. Ch. Longacres Shades of Glory, a stylish Hunting Test winner.

across the wind, seeking scent to locate game, and to stand rigid in its presence. You cannot teach your dog to do this; but it is bred into all GSPs and can be brought out with the right training. I use the word 'training', and you may think I mean 'teaching', but that is not so. Your GSP (referred to as Solo) must learn what his capability is in this sphere of work; but you can give the opportunity to learn. Bereft of that opportunity, he may never come to realise he has it in him.

At some time in his early life, probably between four and twelve months of age, Solo will react to a scent and will 'stand' to it. It may not be to game; his nose is not yet educated. More likely it will a brief scent of a skylark or mouse. It may even be what is referred to as a 'sight point' of a butterfly in the garden or a chicken in the farmyard. In any event, this is the time to seriously begin his pointing education. Most dogs learn to point easily. Soft words of encouragement, holding your youngster gently in check, taking care that initially he does not flush the 'game', will help him to learn. Pointing opportunities can be contrived with the use of caged birds hidden in undergrowth, or, if you are clever enough, by taking a homing pigeon and, after first 'dizzying' it, place it in cover, where it will remain for some time or until disturbed. In these circumstances, be sure that the bird is hidden. Solo needs to progress as soon as possible to using his nose rather than his eyes to find and locate the game. I have read that some old Pointer men used a piece of bread on a string, moving it slowly in front of the dog. The use of a bird wing on a fishing line, tantalisingly whisked away from the inquisitive puppy and left lying still when the puppy is still, is also a popular way of teaching the dog that if he stands on point, the 'game' stays put, but that if he rushes in, it is lost.

WILD GAME

To my mind, there is no substitute for the real thing. I believe it is preferable where possible to run Solo in natural conditions, letting him find his potential on wild game. Young pheasants can often be found along a hedgerow or woodside, but partridges are best of all for initial training. Dogs brought up to point partridges rarely fail on pheasants or grouse, but the reverse is not always true. Partridges are thought to have a very delicate scent compared with other game, so the GSP learning to appreciate them finds the others easy to come to terms with. However, hunting for partridges is not so desirable if you have no control over your GSP.

Your dog is likely to come into contact with hares on good partridge ground and it is too easy to let him get into the habit of chasing whatever is flushed. It is for this reason that I advocate teaching retrieving obediences in parallel with hunting. If Solo is absolutely obedient to the "Stop" whistle, taught in basic and retrieving lessons, he can encounter game in a natural way but will never be out of control. You can allow freedom to run and hunt, confident that your dog will stop to your command, whatever the temptation.

STEADINESS

The retrieving processes should always be kept quite separate from hunting and game-finding in the first year of Solo's life. As he comes to some degree of competence with pointing, let him think that the flush is the end of the exercise. However, if my advised system of retrieving training is followed, Solo will be steady to a thrown dummy or to flushed game, so will have no desire to do other than watch it away. Only when you are confident that Solo is absolutely steady to flushed game and is also steady to thrown dummies and shot, should the whole progression of hunting, pointing, flushing, shooting and retrieving be finally put together – and that should be in the second season of your dog's life. Then you will have every chance of owning a GSP which will be a credit, and a great source of sporting pleasure, to you for all the years of his working life.

ABOVE: Fred Musslewhite's GSPs on a grouse moor: Although GSPs are run singly in trials in the UK, they do 'back' or 'honour' another dog's point naturally when working with other dogs.

RIGHT: When suddenly acknowledging close game scent, some GSPs will lie prone on point, but notice the head is still held high.

VARIATIONS OF POINTING

There are three descriptive terms applied to pointing. A *'productive' point* is one from which game is produced. An *'unproductive' point* is the outcome of a dog pointing residual scent, which remains where game has recently been. While Solo is a youngster, he may not readily distinguish between real and residual scent, but the latter inevitably fades with time and as experience grows the dog will recognise this and break from the point. The dog will usually go forward to the spot and with nose down and tail wagging will indicate that the game has departed.

Lastly, there is a *'false' point*. The dog will suddenly stand as on point, firm as a rock and will, after a few seconds, break off and resume hunting, as if nothing had happened. It may be that a tiny and isolated pocket of air scent suddenly came to the dog, and was gone as soon as it came, leaving no indication of its source. Occasionally, dogs get into the habit of remaining on point in such circumstances. This is undesirable as obviously there can be no positive result. Indeed, in Field Trials a persistent dog is penalised for time-wasting.

STICKING ON POINT

Steadiness at the point is essential. Solo must learn to hold the game at the point without moving. If he edges forward unnecessarily, the wary birds may flush before the gun gets up and the chance is lost. After all, the dog's task is to enhance the possibility of shooting, not to make it impossible. A dog which flushes birds away before commanded to do so is better left at home, as is one which chases after the game when it is flushed – the latter case is another lesson in the importance of the stop whistle.

Young dogs are sometimes loath to flush the game; this is called 'sticking on point'. It is as if the dog and the quarry are in a trance and the commands are unheeded. It is not desirable to let the tendency develop to become a regular occurrence, but do not let this problem worry you too much when Solo is first learning about his pointing capabilities. It is quite likely that he will cease to be 'sticky' on point as his experience grows.

But if your dog maintains this fault, refusing to flush on command, there are two ways of overcoming the problem. The first, and often successful ploy is to walk away from the dog and then recall him with the whistle command. Few, if any, dogs will leave a point without first making the flush. The second method is invariably effective after several repeated experiences. You should go up beside Solo on point, and give the command to flush. If he steadfastly ignores the command, then you must go in front and flush the game yourself. Now Solo realises that he has missed out, and after letting you go forward to the flush a few times he will inevitably go forward with you. Once he is doing so, the slightest move forward, perhaps just the movement of one foot, made by you when you give the flush command, will galvanise him into action and he will go in without hesitation. Give praise for correct action, and he will soon learn to obey your 'flush' command.

STANDING OFF AND CLOSE POINTING

The distance at which dogs point depends on the strength of the scent and the quality of the individual dog's 'nose'. If Solo has 'a good nose', he may well acknowledge game at 100 yards or more on a good scenting day. He can road the scent line, going directly towards the game and hardening on to point at ten yards. But he will please you more if, having acknowledged the game at long distance, he continues to quarter, remaking the acknowledgement every time he crosses the scent line, and only making the firm point when he is within twenty yards or so of the game. If he works like this, he ensures that he, you, and whatever other guns there may be, do not walk forward across ground which has not been hunted over.

Do not expect such sophisticated behaviour from a novice dog; but you will be surprised how quickly a good dog can work this out with practical experience. Conversely, the scenting conditions may be poor, a cold, blustery wind all but destroying the scent. On such a day Solo may not get scent until he is almost on top of the game and may come to a halt from a fast hunting pace, slamming on his brakes, as it were, and pointing within a few feet only of the game. It is then that Solo is most likely to actually lie prone on point (if he has the tendency, which not all do), and if the birds move, will almost slide forward on his belly, rather than regain his feet. It is a habit not encouraged by most Pointer men, although it is more common in Setters. Excepting that Solo may be more difficult to see if he lies prone in cover, there is not, to my mind, less intensity to the point, nor is the outcome less effective.

TRUST

One other thing for you to remember is that Solo, once trained and experienced, is infinitely more efficient than you when it comes to game-finding. Help him by all means within your power, but give him chance to show you what he can do, and place your trust in him. When he indicates that a particular patch of cover does, or does not, hold game, accept that he knows better than you, and that he will almost invariably be right. Nevertheless, be prepared to forgive him if he is just occasionally proved wrong: he is a fallible animal, just as human beings are. Never expect that you can switch your dog on and off, like a machine. Even the best dogs can have an off day or make a mistake sometimes. But once trained and experienced, the errors will be very rare.

BEING PREPARED

This is an opportune moment to reiterate the importance of your dog's physical fitness and sense of well-being. The physical demands on a GSP on a hunting day can be tremendous. Do ensure that Solo gets sufficient high-quality food and has been trained to hard work before thrusting him into the activities of a shooting season. Also, at the end of a shooting day, ensure that he is dry, well fed and able to rest comfortably. A good dog is worth the best care you can give.

Chapter Nine

RETRIEVING

INTRODUCTION

Retrieving is an essential aspect of you GSP's work schedule. In some countries all Pointers and Setters are required to retrieve, but in Britain the specialist dogs have been kept pure and asked only to do the job for which they were bred. Only the Continental pointing breeds are also required to retrieve. Most people who own and shoot over GSPs know that they must be capable of retrieving fur and feather from land or water, *tenderly*. That last word is important for two reasons. Firstly, and quite naturally of course, the game must not be damaged so that it is spoilt for the table. Secondly, when it comes to field trials, the rules require that the game shall be retrieved tenderly, and the penalty for not doing so is elimination!

HARD MOUTH

The GSP was given a reputation for being hard-mouthed by those traditionalists who did not welcome the introduction of the breed to the British shooting scene immediately after the Second World War. The fact is that they are no more hard-mouthed than the Labrador or Golden Retriever. However, it is partly true that the question is not considered in quite the same light in Germany, and it might well be true that some of the early imports may have been harder on the game than desirable. The tendency to hard mouth can be hereditary, but I believe that it is primarily due to over-enthusiasm on the part of the individual dog. If a young and eager dog is sent to retrieve a running wounded cock pheasant, or a wounded live hare, it can be hurt quite badly by being kicked and scratched as it attempts to pick up the game. The dog's natural reaction is to bite hard and kill the game before retrieving it. The next time a dog goes to retrieve, the instinct is to ensure that the bad experience does not recur, so the dog "kills" the game again, and this becomes a habit. Be sure to avoid this situation in early training. An over-excitable dog is also more likely to be hard on game than a phlegmatic one, and dogs that are trained gently and carefully are, in my experience, less likely to be hard-mouthed.

To examine for hard-mouth in field trials the regulations advise: "Place the game on the palm of the hand, breast upward, head forward, and feel the ribs with finger and thumb. They should be round and firm. If they are caved in or flat this is evidence of hard mouth. Superficial gashes due to a difficult capture or lack of experience in capturing a runner by a young dog do not indicate hard mouth. Judges should be sure that the damage has not been caused by the shot or fall."

RETRIEVE TRAINING

Training to retrieve is different from hunting and pointing in that dogs are not working entirely to

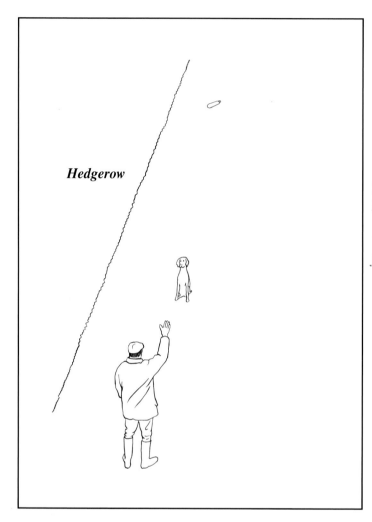

Hedgerow

TEACHING
HAND
SIGNALS
"Go back and
fetch."

their instincts. They are doing something purely because you are asking them to, and should be encouraged to do it and enjoy it, *with* you and *for* you.

Once you feel that Solo has settled in to his new home and looks upon you as his master, you can begin 'fun' training to teach controlled retrieving along with basic Obedience. Remember always that a puppy's power of concentration is very limited and even play lessons should not be longer than a few minutes each session. Initial training is carried out using canvas dummies They can be covered with fur or have pheasant wings attached if desired, to increase their similarity to the real thing. It is personal whim, but I like to see an eight-week-old puppy showing his natural instinct by carrying a dead pigeon or partridge. Do not make a habit of this – once or twice is enough – but it does demonstrate that the puppy is a natural retriever. Also the presence of feathers is accepted in the dog's mind and does not become a problem later.

I am aware that all dogs can be force-trained to retrieve; it is even claimed by some that dogs so trained are more reliable than natural retrievers. Nevertheless, I advocate ensuring at an early age that your puppy has a natural bent for retrieving and that he will pick up and carry whatever comes to hand – or rather mouth! Let your puppy play with and carry about any toys you choose, or an old slipper, but do not use these things for his retrieve training. Your dog should understand that what he retrieves to you is yours and not his. It is highly prized by you and he is privileged to be allowed to retrieve it, but it is not his to keep, chew or play with.

Make the first week of retrieve training really easy. You will find that if you go to the end of the garden and throw a dummy towards the house, the puppy's kennel or bed, he will be more likely to go to his 'refuge' with it, rather than come to the strange end of the garden to bring it to you. But if you throw the dummy away from the house or bed, then he will instinctively return there with it. Once Solo has grasped the basic principle of picking up the dummy and returning to you with it, cease asking him to do simple, seen retrieves altogether. If you do throw a dummy and ask the puppy to be steady and await your command before retrieving it, be sure at least that it is hidden in some simple cover so that he has to use his nose to find it. Only let Solo retrieve about a third of the dummies you throw in this manner. Let him get accustomed to sitting and watching you fetch them yourself. Never let a dog fail in an attempted retrieve – that is not good for self-confidence.

If you realise that Solo is unable to find the dummy, go forward immediately and help him to succeed. Discard the repetitive use of seen dummy retrieves as soon as the puppy has mastered their execution. This type of retrieving does not encourage steadiness. However careful you may be to ensure that Solo sits, stays and waits for the retrieve command, he will soon learn the order of events and, knowing the final outcome, will anticipate, and will want to make the retrieve before being commanded to do so.

MEMORY AND BLIND RETRIEVES
Now is the time to introduce the 'memory retrieve', a method of retrieving which Solo will not only enjoy thoroughly, but which will go a long way to ensuring that he will be steady when he is adult. The process is as follows. Take the dummy, with Solo walking to heel – on a lead if necessary – and toss the dummy a few yards into some long grass or similar cover. As Solo watches the flight and fall of the dummy, give the command "Leave", and walk away with him. Go only ten or so yards the first time; sit Solo facing you with his back to the dummy, release the lead and give the command "Go back and fetch", at the same time thrusting your open, up-held left hand forward, as if to push open a door. Your puppy may go straight back, but if not and if the pup is confused, run back with him, repeating the command and, if necessary, showing where the dummy lies.

After only a few experiences, Solo will grasp the idea and will go back to where he remembers the dummy is, to make the retrieve. You may be surprised at how quickly he will learn this lesson and how much fun he will derive from doing it. Lengthen the distance as you progress, eventually reaching the point where you can sit your dog 200 yards from the dummy; leave him and go another 100 yards from him before you turn and repeat the words and action that will signal him to effect the retrieve.

As the months go by you can progress from memory retrieves to unseen 'blind' retrieves as an extension of this retrieve system. Execute a reasonably simple memory retrieve twice in exactly the same place and then, unseen by your dog, leave the dummy in the same place yet again. Go through the process as if it were a memory retrieve and when you give the command, Solo will go back, remembering what he has just done, and find the dummy.

If you have asked too much, go back with him again and help him to succeed at the retrieve Again, you may be surprised at how soon he will get the idea and how efficient he will progressively become at doing memory and blind retrieves. Never send Solo back for a memory or blind retrieve unless there is a dummy there for him to find. He must go back because he has absolute faith in you – and that faith must never be broken.

RECAPITULATION

Now let us look at what Solo has learned and what you and he have achieved. Firstly, instead of the progression, throw, fall, sit, stay, retrieve – which is easy to break – he has learned throw, fall, mark, walk away, sit, retrieve. He has accepted that when he sees a potential retrieve, instead of anticipating the command to retrieve and running in, he must actually walk away from the dummy before he can go to retrieve it: the exact opposite of running in! Additionally, he has learned to mark and remember the point of fall; he has learned the "Get back" signal and command, even when at distance from you, which will be useful countless times in the field.

An old dog of ours, Midlander the Cisco Kid, has recently died. He was trained exclusively by this method. He never ran in to fall in all his life, though he picked many hundreds of birds (Mic and I once picked up at a shoot with Cisco and one other bitch where 1300 birds were shot in three days). When I threw a dummy, or he saw a bird shot, he would glance at the point of fall and turn away, despite being desperately eager, completely accepting the fact that he had to walk away before he could make the retrieve. Naturally, in Field Trial competitions, you do not go through the process of walking away. The dog might be surprised but will still effect the retrieve on command. Providing the habit is not broken regularly, it will not affect training.

DIRECTIONAL CONTROL

Control of your dog in the field is an important aspect of retrieve training. It is essential that Solo goes out on a line indicated by you with a wave of your arm to seek a blind retrieve. He must stop on command at distance and go left, right, back or toward you according to the command given. He must understand the command "Hi Lost" as meaning "That is the area, now use your initiative and find the retrieve". Once making the retrieve, Solo must not be distracted by other occurrences; another bird or a running rabbit. He must bring the bird to hand directly, not putting it down (other than possibly to get a better hold) and must treat it tenderly.

The basic training for this work has been covered. Commonsense must play a big part in your approach to your dog. Stretch his capability or it will not grow, but do not expect miracles overnight, and never forget that progressive learning depends on understanding and on repetition.

When initially practising memory and blind retrieves, do these back along the line of a hedge or fence in order that Solo may more easily recognise that he has to go back in a straight line. When sending away for a blind retrieve, be sure to put the dog slightly on the downwind side of the dummy or bird. The chance of success is much higher if Solo has the chance to scent the retrieve. Remember that he is using his nose to locate it. If he goes upwind he will not 'see' the dummy, however near to it he may be.

DOUBLE AND MULTIPLE RETRIEVES AND DISTRACTIONS

There should be no difficulty in sending your dog for a second retrieve immediately after the first, but in a different direction. Begin this training sitting Solo in front of you, about 20 yards away. Throw two dummies, one to his left and one to his right. Now, by using the "Go left – go right" command, you can send him for one of them. If he goes the wrong way, stop him with the whistle command and repeat the signal, perhaps going a bit nearer to him. Encourage Solo to bring the dummy directly back to you. Sit him again in the same spot and send him for the second dummy.

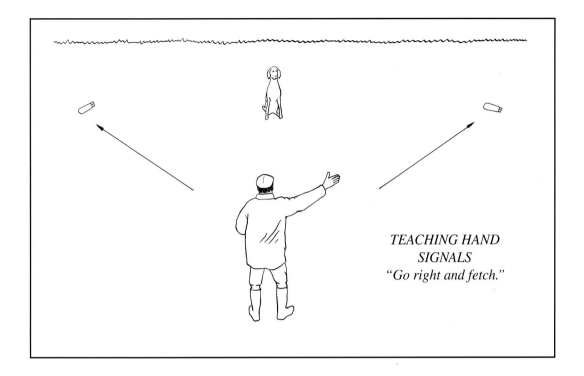

*TEACHING HAND
SIGNALS
"Go right and fetch."*

As his competence increases, throw a distraction dummy to one side as he comes in with a retrieve, but teach him to leave this and to complete the retrieve.

In early training stages, do not send Solo for the distraction dummy afterwards. Eventually you should be able to put out an unseen dummy, then send him for a seen retrieve – not in the same direction – and send him for the unseen one afterwards. All the directional field control signals you have taught him will come into use in these exercises. You can even extend the lesson to the retrieving of five or six dummies, one after the other. This is exactly what Solo may have to do when, as a trained dog, he goes with you to pick up at a formal shoot.

WATER RETRIEVES

A good dog should be as capable a retriever in water as on land. You do not need to teach Solo to swim, only to introduce him to water in a way that does not unnerve him. For a dog, swimming requires the same movement as walking on land. As a youngster Solo can play in shallow water, perhaps following an older dog; and he will walk into water on a lead with you with a bit of encouragement. Providing he is eager to retrieve, Solo will go into water to do so and will swim when the water gets deep enough. His efforts will be unsophisticated at first, but as soon as he has a dummy in his mouth he will swim smoothly and will soon master the technique.

If you have trouble at introduction to water, take Solo into shallow water on the lead and gradually walk him to deeper water. You will get wet up to the thighs, so be prepared. Keep moving, and in that depth of water Solo will have to swim to be with you. Walk him about for a minute or two; do it maybe several times until he begins to get confidence. Then, while you are

Ft.Ch. Loveday's Kathleen, owned by Fred Musslewhite, retrieving a live pheasant from water!

together in water and Solo is swimming, toss a dummy a few yards, slip the lead and send him for it. I have never known this to fail, and careful progression will soon have the dog making simple seen retrieves from the bank. In early training, avoid places where the access is difficult.

BLIND RETRIEVES ACROSS WATER

Open and All-Aged Stakes Field Trials in the UK require a blind retrieve to be executed from across water without a shot being fired. I have heard it said that it is an unnecessary 'circus act', but this is not so. On several occasions, at the end of the day, I have encountered the situation where a bird has been shot and has landed across water and the shooter has no dog – at least no dog capable of effecting the retrieve. Success in this instance is achieved providing the following method of teaching is adhered to exactly – assuming your dog is already competent at simple retrieves from water.

   You will need a helper. Go to a river or canal where the water is deep enough but not too wide. Throw the dummy to the other side of the water for Solo to see. Let him make the retrieve. Repeat this in exactly the same place twice more. He now knows, and is confident he can do that retrieve. Let your helper now cover Solo's eyes. Throw the dummy exactly as before, and he will hear it fly through the air and hit the ground. Remove the blindfold and send the dog to retrieve, always remembering the command: "Get across and fetch". This time, or maybe when the exercise is repeated the next day, Solo will go across and fetch the dummy. Repeat the whole lesson every day for a week, in the same spot each time, and Solo will effect the unseen retrieve easily.

The next step is to take Solo to the same place again, but this time, after performing the seen retrieve twice, let the helper walk away with Solo until he cannot see or hear the dummy being thrown. Bring the dog back immediately and send him for the retrieve. Repeat this for a week or so until Solo has learned the lesson thoroughly and has complete faith that there will be a retrieve for him when he goes at your command across the water. Now you can repeat the lesson several times, going to different places. Never, never, send Solo across water unless there is a retrieve to find. The whole process is based on your dog's faith in your integrity – never break it.

RETRIEVING RUNNERS

Although GSPs have a penchant for tracking blood scent, some training in this aspect of work is necessary. Regrettably, this is often overlooked, to the detriment of the dog's performance in the field. Efficiency in tracking wounded birds is a very important requirement of any retrieving dog, if not *the* most important. These are the birds a good dog can bring to the bag, rather than leave to a fox – quite apart from observing the rule that sportsmen do not leave wounded game unpicked.

A scent trail must be laid for Solo to follow, but this must not be observed by the dog. A dead rabbit or game bird should be dragged on a line, not always a straight line. It is then desirable in training to ensure that the carcase leaves a little blood on the course. This is best done with two people dragging the 'retrieve' between them. In this way, the trail is free from the handler's own scent. Leave the retrieve at the end of the trail. Ensure that there is good scent, and a little blood

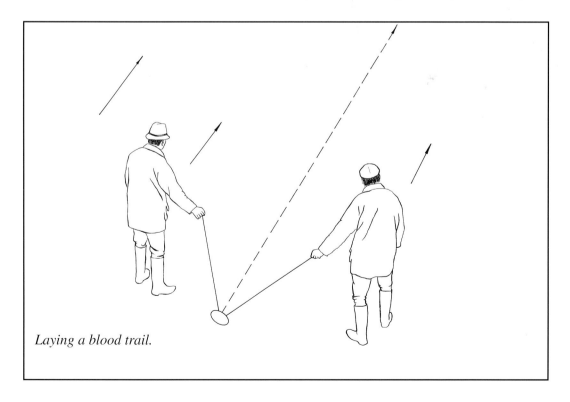

Laying a blood trail.

A grouse to hand: David Layton trialing Midlander Oriental Ranee.

left at the starting point. Bring Solo back to the start and encourage him to pick up the scent. Use the command "High Lost" or "Seek – Fetch", and set him off to follow the trail. If Solo has good natural ability, he may well go straight to the retrieve, but initially it is advisable to have the dog on a long leash, in order to correct his line if he goes astray or appears to lose the scent. Praise Solo for success, and progress by making subsequent trails more difficult – turning corners, going through hedges, even across a narrow stream.

Although you are asking Solo to use his nose to find the 'runner', he is not taking air scent; in fact, air scent would be a distraction to the purpose of the exercise. Be careful, therefore, to lay the trail downwind – with the wind behind you as you walk. This will make the task easier for Solo to find the ground scent he must follow.

DISTRACTION OF LIVE GAME

At some time in his life Solo will go out and retrieve shot game, and while doing so will come upon live game. Solo may ignore it and complete the retrieve, in which case you may never be aware of it! Much more likely, he will stop and point. The purists would say that the dog is not doing his job properly; he was sent to retrieve and that is what he should do.

A pheasant retrieved to hand: Ernie Wheeler trialing Ft.Ch. Hurlston Wheelwood Commander.

Nevertheless, on a rough shooting day when Solo has worked hard, but as yet has no birds in the bag, it is reasonable that you should be delighted when your dog offers you two birds instead of one. You may be happy that Solo should flush this second bird on command and retrieve both of them in turn. Many Field Trial judges would agree with you! In a case like this, or indeed, any other time when Solo is on point, do not try to call him away if it can be avoided. After all, he is doing the very job for which he has been bred and trained. If a Field Trial judge insists, then gently pull Solo off point with a lead if possible, go beyond the point area and send Solo for the initial retrieve. Do not try to explain to the dog why you did this – he will not understand!

POINTING WOUNDED GAME

The only time you should call Solo in when he is pointing is if he has been sent for a retrieve This may be a frequent occurrence with a young dog, and the likelihood is that the game is still alive. Often Solo will realise after a moment that this is the case and will pick up the bird, particularly after a few words of encouragement. Otherwise, if you call Solo in, he is unlikely to come away without the retrieve, and will pick it before he comes back to you. It is a habit which experienced dogs soon relinquish.

AT A DRIVEN SHOOT

Picking up at a driven shoot can be good experience training for young Solo, providing he is not given the opportunity to ignore the lessons already taught. Always try to position yourself to see and retrieve the difficult ones; the birds that have glided back or have been pricked and will never fly again. These are the birds Solo will learn most from, in addition to being the ones the keeper will appreciate.

Leave the easy, dead birds which will lie on the grass near the guns for them to pick! GSPs can turn their hand to driven bird shooting, and if quite steady, can stand with you at the peg if you are shooting. But this is not the forte of utility gundogs, and although there are odd occasions when their nose may be better than a Labrador's, they do not compete with these specialist gundogs at the task of 'mopping up'.

POSTSCRIPT

Retrieving is an essential, but ancillary aspect of a pointing dog's life. The sole object of training Solo to be a competent retriever is, firstly, to find and retrieve wounded game so that it may be despatched as quickly and as humanely as possible; secondly, to put all the shot game in the bag promptly in order to resume hunting. That hunting ability, which is certainly the great strength of your German Shorthaired Pointer is, hopefully, the prime reason why you acquired one of this breed in the first place!

Chapter Ten

THE VERSATILE GSP

WILDFOWLING

The art of duck and goose shooting has long been a food-producing sport in most countries of the world. Whether for the great migratory flights across the vastness of North America, the daily flights to and from coastal mud-flats to inland feeding grounds, or the decoying of wildfowl on the smallest of pools – in all these situations a dog to retrieve the shot fowl is an essential asset. Certainly many GSP owners are wildfowlers on and off, and their dogs do the job competently, though restricted to the retrieving role.

The GSP should work equally well on land and in the water, and the breed's short coat can be cleaned and dried with ease.

Extreme cold is often an adjunct to goose or duck shooting, including the privation of waiting for hours in a muddy hide for the birds to flight in. GSPs have a hunting instinct and they love it, always eager to fill the bag: However, it has to be said that their short and relatively thin coat does not fit them ideally for the task. One thing to remember, especially when wildfowling, but at other times also, is that at the end of the day, a very wet dog needs to be dried off reasonably before setting off for the journey home. A 'chamois' leather will make an ideal towel for your Shorthair. One distinct advantage of the GSP's short coat is the ease with which your dog can be dried and cleaned. Many times in our early association with GSPs, when small local dog shows were popular, we would go to our nearby game-shooting ground in the morning and get truly wet and muddy before noon, but take the same dogs to the dog show in the afternoon 'all cleaned and polished' without difficulty. I fancy that you could not hope to do that with a Spaniel!

FALCONRY

The training and use of free-flying falcons, hawks and eagles to catch game for food has been a sport in Europe and the Middle East for many centuries. There has been a recent revival, especially in the UK, and many who follow this pastime use a pointing dog. Traditionally, Pointers were, and sometimes still are, used; but as the falconer may want to hunt and flush birds from cover, the versatility of the GSP makes it admirable for the job.

Surprisingly, the dog is not upset by the falcon stooping to take what the dog has produced. GSPs fall very easily into the working ways of raptors – either falcons circling high in the sky, or even huge eagles flown from the fist at hares or rabbits. They seem to enjoy the sport just as much as hunting and shooting, even though deprived of the retrieve.

Most falconer's dogs are used exclusively for that job of work, trained to accept the role of the bird, hunting, pointing and flushing the game for it. But more conventionally trained gundogs can turn a hand to it if given the opportunity. I am not a falconer, but on occasions have been invited to work my dogs for friends who are. I have always been pleasantly surprised at the ease with which the dogs adapted to the task. I remember once working a dog for a man with a Bonneli's Eagle. I had some worry that the bitch might react badly to that giant of a bird. Not so, the GSP was not in the least apprehensive about the bird, which is more than I could say about myself!

The modus operandi of the sport is fascinating, approached normally in one of three ways, according to the type of raptor and the game to be hunted. The very beautiful but minute Merlin is flown at skylarks and pippits. I have no experience in this field. I believe Peregrines and Lanners are used to hunt partridges and pheasants, and sometimes rabbits. The dog hunts to find the game and points, holding it. The falcon is cast off and circles to find a thermal on which to climb to 400 or 500 feet. The overhead presence of the falcon holds the game more tightly in situ, as it is aware of the threat and afraid to fly. When the bird reaches its 'waiting on' height it is usually slightly up-wind of the game, in order to dive (or stoop, as it is called) down-wind when the birds are flushed. The falcon drops at incredible speed, with almost completely closed wings, only levelling out at the last second to take the quarry. Harris hawks often 'wait on' high in a tree, and will take partridge or pheasant. Goshawks are traditionally flown 'off the fist', as are eagles. The bigger eagles appear to be quite slow when they are cast off. It is an illusion: they are successfully flown at hares, rabbits and the smaller deer.

I believe the sport of falconry is, unfortunately, not legal in New Zealand or Australia.

DEER STALKING

The European utility gundogs are all used as deer stalkers' dogs in their respective countries of origin at least, but also to some extent in the UK. The main task for the dog is to follow the blood scent of a wounded animal in order to locate its hiding place in the forest. Some dogs are trained to give tongue at finding the beast, keeping it at bay until the stalker approaches to despatch it.

A remarkable method of search is implemented by hanging a wooden baton on a thong round the dog's neck – just long enough for the dog to be able to run, but also to be able to take it in the mouth. When the hunter loses a wounded beast, he sends the dog off to find it by following the scent. The deer may have gone miles rather than yards, and if the dog is unsuccessful the dog returns with the baton still hanging free. But when the quarry is found, the dog immediately takes the baton in the mouth and so returns to the stalker. Knowing then that the dog has been successful, the stalker follows his clever canine companion back to where the beast lies. This is quite a different role for the dog to play, compared with the traditional hunt, point and retrieve one, but it is one at which GSPs are known to be very efficient. A good GSP can be expected to successfully track a blood scent even when it may be twenty-four hours old, so the contribution made by the dog can be a valuable one.

A GSP accompanying a deer stalker can often offer another bonus. The dog may scent the immediate presence of deer, and indicate it by attitude, long before the stalker would otherwise be aware. This may considerably increase the chance of the stalker getting a shot at his quarry.

DRUG AND EXPLOSIVES LOCATION
German Shorthaired Pointers are not employed as police dogs in the normally accepted sense; but they are selected by security forces, after suitable training, to use their incredibly good scenting powers to find drugs and explosives. Contrary to popular belief, I am assured that dogs sniffing for drugs do not become addicted. As these very words are written, comes news that two GSPs have commenced work with the security staff at London's Heathrow Airport!

Chapter Eleven

THE GSP IN NORTH AMERICA

USA: PART I: THE SHOW SCENE

INTRODUCTION

Just as it would be impossible to make a success of a book without the help of all those who contribute photographs, so it is with information which must, necessarily, be outside the author's personal experience. It is my very good fortune, however, to list amongst my closest friends, Ken and Marybeth Kirkland, of Maidens, Va. We really got to know one another very well when Marybeth was Show Secretary of the 1992 GSP Nationals, and the Mason Dixon GSP Club Specialty, both shows being staged back to back during the same week of May in Frederick, Md. This lady really 'came of age' at that double event! I am full of admiration for her organising ability and staying power. I had the great pleasure of judging the M/D Club Sweepstakes (males), and went over some 75 youngsters as well as seeing something like 650 GSPs at the show venue.

We had not visited the US before, and believed, like most other GSP fanciers in the UK, that the American representatives of the breed were too big. My pleasure was increased, therefore, to see that, on the showing of those 650 dogs, by and large the breed in the US is no more oversize than in the UK. Rightfully, and by reason of the number of serious breeders, there are many excellent specimens in the US, and there must be some pretty hot photographers too, judging by the shots I have been sent!

It is heartening to realise that the aspirations of GSP owners and breeders are virtually the same wherever they are encountered. The broad principle of keeping the breed pure, and breeding to produce stock which can do the job for which it is intended, is as surely the common aim in the United States of America as it is in Germany and in the United Kingdom. The fact that there are some differences in procedures at shows or in the field, matters little. Perhaps it is more difficult to make up Champions by the rules laid down in the UK: certainly one can see good reasons for dogs being horseback-handled in the US. These factors are ones which have emerged to suit the people and the conditions of the different countries. They certainly do not change the basic type and nature of the German Shorthaired Pointer. Marybeth Kirkland has been a wonderful source of information. There was a lot of work involved for her and I can only hope it was a labour of love (for the breed, not the author!).

STATUS AND BREEDING

Out of the huge number of reputable breeders in the US, the following details are no more than a representative sample of the whole. There is little doubt that the GSP has really taken off in

America. After stabilizing itself as a hunter's breed par excellence in the early days, additional popularity has grown tremendously for the breed as a show dog and companion dog. Georgina Byrne (*Der Deutsch Kurzhaar* 1989) lists about 130 established breeders in the US. There are some sixty GSP breed clubs, mostly identifying with the States in which they flourish, under the umbrella of The German Shorthaired Pointer Club of America. The monthly magazine of the GSPCA, *Shorthair*, must be one of the best specialist breed publications of any breed, anywhere in the world. Put all that together and it spells one word – success. If ever a national breed of one country can be said to have been 'adopted' by another, then it must be the German Shorthaired Pointer in the United States of America.

The story started in 1925 when a GSP bitch was imported from Austria to the mid-west state of Montana, by a Dr C.Thornton, and as enthusiastic hunters of the area discovered the remarkable versatility of this dog, the popularity of the breed grew rapidly. The breed was admitted to the American Kennel Club Stud Book in March 1930. It was not until the 1940s, however, that the GSPCA received its Charter, and it was May 1946 before the breed club officially approved the Standard for the GSP, adapted from the German version, with only minor variations.

CHAMPIONSHIP SHOWS
The rules of the American Kennel Club provide a basis for the organisation of Championship shows at which AKC registered dogs may compete to gain awards which entitle them to points towards Championship status. With permission of the AKC, the pertinent parts of those rules are reproduced.

CLASSIFICATIONS
SECTION 1: Lists the breeds which may be exhibited. German Shorthaired Pointers are included in Group 1 – Sporting Dogs. (In the UK they would be referred to as Gundogs.)
SECTION 2: No class shall be provided for any dog under six months of age except at sanctioned matches when approved by the American Kennel Club.
SECTION 3: The regular classes of the American Kennel Club shall be as follows:
Puppy; Twelve-to-Eighteen months; Novice; Bred-by-Exhibitor; American-bred; Open; Winners. These classes shall be divided by sex.
SECTION 4: The Puppy class shall be for dogs that are over six months but under twelve months, that are not Champions. The age of a dog shall be calculated up to and inclusive of the first day of a show. For example, a dog whelped on January 1st is eligible to complete in a puppy class at a show the first day of which is July 1st of the same year and may continue to compete in puppy classes at shows up to and including a show the first day of which is the 31st day of December of the same year; but is not eligible to compete in a puppy class at a show the first day of which is January 1st of the following year. The first day of a show is considered to be the first day on which there is regular conformation judging.
SECTION 5: The Twelve-to-Eighteen Month class shall be for dogs that are twelve months of age and over, but under eighteen months, that are not Champions. The age of a dog shall be calculated up to and inclusive of the first day of a show. For instance, a dog whelped on January 1st is eligible to compete in a class at a show the first day of which is January 1st of the following year, and may continue to compete in this class at shows up to and including a show the first day of which is the 30th day of June of that year; but is not eligible to compete in this class at a show the first day of which is July 1st of that year.
SECTION 6: The Novice class shall be for dogs six months of age and over, whelped in the

United States of America, Canada or Mexico which have not, prior to the date of closing of entries, won three first prizes in the Novice class, a first prize in Bred-by-Exhibitor, American-bred or Open classes, nor one or more points towards their championship.

SECTION 7: The Bred-by-Exhibitor class shall be for dogs whelped in the United States of America, or, if individually registered in the American Kennel Club Stud Book, for dogs whelped in Canada or Mexico, that are six months of age and over, that are not Champions and that are owned wholly or in part by the person or by the spouse of the person who was the breeder or one of the breeders of record.

Dogs entered in this class must be handled in the class by the breeder or one of the breeders of record, or by a member of the immediate family of the breeder or one of the breeders of record. For purposes of this section, the members of an immediate family are: husband, wife, father, mother, son, daughter, brother, sister.

SECTION 8: The American-bred class shall be for all dogs (except Champions) six months of age and over, whelped in the United States of America, by reason of a mating which took place in the United States of America.

SECTION 9: The Open class shall be for any dog six months of age or over except in a member Specialty club show held only for American-bred dogs, in which case the Open class shall be only for American-bred dogs.

SECTION 10: The Winners class shall be divided by sex and each division shall be open only to undefeated dogs of the same sex which have won first prizes in either the Puppy, Twelve-to-Eighteen Month, Novice, Bred-by-Exhibitor, American-bred or Open classes. There shall be no entry fee for entry in the Winners class. After the Winners prize has been awarded in one of the sex divisions, the second prize-winning dog, if undefeated except by the dog awarded Winners, shall compete with the other eligible dogs for Reserve Winners. No eligible dog may be withheld from competition.

Winners class shall be allowed only at shows where American-bred and Open classes shall be given. A member Specialty club holding a show for American-bred dogs only may include Winners classes, provided the necessary regular classes are included in the classification. A member club holding a show with restricted entries may include Winners classes, provided the necessary regular classes are included in the classification.

SECTION 11: No Winners class, or any class resembling it, shall be given at sanctioned matches.

SECTION 12. A club that provides Winners classes shall also provide Competition for Best of Breed or for Best of Variety in those breeds for which varieties are provided in this chapter. The awards in this competition shall be Best of Breed or Best of Variety in Breed.

The following categories of dogs may be entered in this competition:

Dogs that are Champions of Record.

Dogs which according to their owner's records have completed the requirements for a championship but whose championships are unconfirmed.

The showing of dogs whose Championships are unconfirmed is limited to a period of 90 days from the date of show where a dog completed the requirements for a Championship according to the owner's records.

In addition, the Winners dog and Winners bitch, together with any undefeated dogs that have competed at the show only in additional non-regular classes shall compete for Best of Breed or Best of Variety of Breed. If the Winners dog or Winners bitch is awarded Best of Breed or Best of Variety of Breed, it shall be automatically awarded Best of Winners; otherwise the Winners dog and Winners bitch shall be judged together for Best of Winners following the judging of Best of

Breed or Best of Variety of Breed. The dog awarded Best of Winners shall be credited with the number of points calculated for Winners Dog or Winners Bitch, whichever is the greater. In the event that Winners is awarded only in one sex, there shall be no Best of Winners award.

After Best of Breed or Best of Variety of Breed and Best of Winners have been awarded, the judge shall select Best of Opposite Sex to Best of Breed or Best of Variety of Breed. Eligible for this award are:

Dogs of opposite sex to Best of Breed or Best of Variety of Breed that have been entered for Best of Breed competition. The dog awarded Winners of the opposite sex to the Best of Breed or Best of Variety of Breed. Any undefeated dogs of the opposite sex to Best of Breed or Best of Variety of Breed which have competed at the show only in additional non-regular classes.

A dog that has been defeated in any regular class or non-regular class for single dog entries in its breed or variety at the show, is ineligible to compete for Best of Breed or Variety. A dog that has been defeated by a dog of its own sex in any regular or non-regular class for single dog entries in its breed or variety at the show, is ineligible to compete for Best of Opposite Sex to Best of Breed or Variety.

SHOW DETAILS

In holding a show, a society is bound to provide a schedule of the event, called the Premium List, together with entry forms, at least five weeks before the date of the show. Entries close about three weeks prior to the date of the show. Any prize ribbons or rosettes given in the regular classes must be Blue for First Prize, Red for Second Prize, Yellow for Third Prize and White for Fourth Prize.

A catalogue containing all the relevant details of conditions, judges, as contained in the Premium List, together with the details of all entries and exhibitors; and the schedule of points towards Championship governing each breed in the show, shall be printed by the show organisers.

CHAMPIONSHIP POINTS

SECTION 1: Championship Points will be recorded for Winners Dog and Winners Bitch for each breed listed at licensed or member dog shows approved by the American Kennel Club, provided the certification of the Secretary as described has been printed in the premium list for the show. Championship points will be recorded according to the number of eligible dogs competing in the regular classes of each sex in each breed or variety, and according to the Schedule of Points established by the Board of Directors.

If the dog designated Winners Dog or Winners Bitch is also awarded Best of Breed or Variety, the dogs of both sexes that have been entered for Best of Breed or Variety competition and that have been defeated in such competition, shall be counted in addition to the dogs that competed in the regular classes for its sex in calculating championship points.

If the dog designated Winners Dog or Winners Bitch is also awarded Best of Opposite Sex to Best of Breed or Variety, the dogs of its own sex that have been entered for Best of Breed or Variety competition and that have been defeated in competition for Best of Opposite Sex shall be counted in addition to the dogs that competed in the regular classes for its sex in calculating championship points. The dog awarded Best of Winners shall be credited with the number of points calculated for Winners Dog or Winners Bitch, whichever is greater.

In counting the number of eligible dogs in competition, a dog that is disqualified or that is dismissed, excused or ordered from the ring by the judge, or from which all awards are withheld, shall not be included.

SECTION 2: A dog which in its breed competition at a show shall have been placed Winners and which also shall have won its group class at the same show shall be awarded Championship points figured at the highest point rating of any breed or recognised variety or height of any breed entered in the show and entitled to winners points in its group, or if it also shall have been designated Best in Show, shall be awarded Championship points figured at the highest point rating of any breed or recognised variety or height of any breed entered and entitled to Winners points in the show. The final points to be awarded under this section shall not be in addition to but inclusive of any points previously awarded the dog in its breed competition or under the provisions of this section.

SECTION 3: At shows in which the winner's classes of certain breeds are divided into recognised varieties of those breeds as specified in these Rules and Regulations, the procedure for computing Championship points shall be the same as if each recognised variety were a separate breed.

SECTION 4: Any dog which shall have won fifteen points shall become a Champion of Record, if six or more of said points shall have been won at two shows with a rating of three or more Championship points each and under two different judges, and some one or more of the balance of said points shall have been won under some other judge or judges than the two judges referred to above. A dog becomes a Champion when it is so officially recorded by the American Kennel Club, and when registered in the Stud Book shall be entitled to a championship certificate.

SECTION 5: Any dog which has been awarded the titles of Champion of Record may be designated as a 'Dual Champion' after it has also been awarded the title of Field Champion, but no certificate will be awarded for a Dual Championship. Any dog which has been awarded the titles of Champion of Record, Obedience Trial Champion and Field Champion may be designated as 'Triple Champion', but no certificate will be awarded for a Triple Champion.

THE FIRST CHAMPIONS

The first American Kennel Club (AKC) Show Champions were Becky von Hohenbruck and Baron v d Brickwedde, winning their titles in 1936. Both these dogs were bred by that first importer, and it was to be another four years before another quality specimen, Ch. Sportsman Dream, became the first German Shorthaired Pointer to win an all-breed Best in Show.

The first American dual title for the breed was a solid liver dog, Rusty von Schwarenberg, and he was also the first Field Trial Champion – this was in 1947. By and large, Americans prefer the brighter coated GSPs to the solid livers. Despite this, Rusty managed to earn two Westminster KC Best of Breeds and three Breed Specialties during his show career. Two years later, Schatz v Schwarenberg became the first bitch to gain the title Dual Champion.

THE EARLY YEARS

Prior to the end of World War II, the majority of the support and enthusiasm for the breed came from Mid West and West Coast breeders, who looked upon the breed as a most versatile hunting dog with the added bonus of adequate, if not substantial, qualification as a show dog. It took longer for the breed's reputation as an outstanding hunting companion to develop similarly on the East Coast, and longer still before the GSP flourished in East Coast breed show rings. Today, the East Coast boasts some of the most noted breeders and German Shorthaired Pointers in the world. At the top of the list can be found Ch. Adam von Fuehrerheim, and Am. Can. Ch. Fieldfine's Count Rambard, the first and second top-producing sires of Show Champions, with 115 and 89, respectively.

Much has changed since those exciting beginnings. Sadly, most of the early breeders are no longer in the sport, and their remarkable dogs have fallen off the top of the pedigrees of today's GSPs. Fortunately for the German Shorthaired Pointer enthusiasts in America, the parent club, the

GSPCA, maintains meticulous records, complete with photographs of many of the early specimens. Unlike many other sporting breeds where there is little resemblance between 'field' dog and 'show' dog, German Shorthaired Pointer breeders in the US strive to maintain the dual purpose of the breed.

PRESENT-DAY BREEDERS

Of the great list of successful and reputable breeders and their dogs, it is only possible to survey a small number. The following prefixes are listed in alphabetical order and are no more than a sample of the many highly respected breeders of German Shorthaired Pointers who have become so successful in the United States of America.

KINGSWOOD

Located in New York, this kennel began with the purchase of a solid liver puppy as a pet for the three children of Jim and June Burns. This puppy became Am. Can. Ch. Wentworth's Happy Wanderer CD, an all-time top producer, and after her demise was elected to the GSPCA Hall of Fame. This bitch's influence on the breed can be seen in her production record of fifteen Champions, and an additional seventy or more in the next three generations. Their accomplishments can be seen in the record books, starting with Ch. Kingswood's Night Rider who, at the 1979 National Specialty Show, took Best in Sweepstakes, Best Opposite Sex in Futurity, Winner's Dog and Best of Winners. At the same show, his sister, Ch. Kingswood's Gilda was Best Opposite Sex in Sweepstakes and Reserve Winners Bitch.

In 1980 another solid liver, Ch. Kingswood's Royal Flush took Best in Futurity at the National Specialty. One of her daughters, Ch. Kingswood's Miss Chiff, set a record which still stands today.

June Burns' Ch. Kingswood's Miss Chiff: This bitch made breed history with her outstanding success in the show ring.

June Burns' Ch. Kingswood's Maximilian: A Best in Show winner and a top-producing sire.

Ashbey.

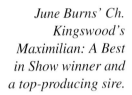

In 1982, at the age of 14 months, she swept the GSPCA National Specialty, taking Best in Futurity, Best in Sweepstakes and Winners Bitch. At the National Specialty the following year, she captured Best of Breed. The year after that, and eight weeks after whelping twelve puppies, she went Best Opp Sex to Best of Breed. These wins were especially sweet for the Burns family because Miss Chiff was the daughter of their own Am. Can. Ch. Kingswood's Windsong.

Am. Can. Ch. Kingswood's Windsong was a Sporting Group winner and the third top German Shorthaired Pointer in 1978. He is on the all-time top producer list with eighteen Champions to his credit. Down from him come a line of top producers, both male and female, including: Ch. Kingswood's Buffy of Geremy; Ch. Kingswood's Maximilian; Ch. Kingswood's Candy Kiss; Ch. Shadywood's Lady v Kingswood; and Ch. Abby Road's Sheana. At the 1981 National Specialty Show his son and daughter took Winner's Dog and Winner's Bitch.

In 1983 Kingswood obtained, on a co-ownership with Linda Bynum, Am. Can. Ch. Weinland's Matinee Idol, now in the GSPCA Hall of Fame. For three years Matt was one of the top show dogs in the US, and a Sporting Group winner in Canada as well. In 1984 Matt won an all-breed Best in Show, owner-handled by Jim. Presently he has 45 Champion get, and is fifth on the all-time top producer list. At the 1985 National Specialty Show, his son, Ch. Kingswood's Maximilian, was Winners Dog at the age of ten months. Max went on to become a top producer himself, with thirty Champions to date. He is the sire of the 1992 National Specialty Show Best of Breed winner, Ch. Sunreach's Flexible Flyer CDX, the High in Trial winner OT Ch. Sunreach's Ticked Tornado, and the combined High in Trial winner, Sunreach Hans v Minden CDX.

Carol Chadwick's Dual Am. and Can. Ch. NMK's Brittania von Sibelstein.

NORTHWOOD MOUNTAIN KENNEL
Known more familiarly as NMK, this kennel began in California in 1978. Carol Chadwick's foundation dog, Am. Can. Ch. NMK's Placer Country Snowbird is the sire of more than forty Show Champions, including the top all-time winning GSP in American history, Dual Ch. and Can. Ch. Brittania v Sibelstein. Known as 'Brit', this bitch's record reads like a *Who's Who* directory. She was the number one German Shorthaired Pointer for two years in 1986 and 1987, top Sporting Dog in the US with forty-nine Best in Shows, and the only GSP to be a Dual Champion, National Specialty Show Best of Breed winner, and multi-Best in Show winner in the history of dogs. Add to this her production of fourteen Show Champions, six with points towards Dual titles, and one can see that this bitch is not only outstanding in her own right but will be a strong influence in the breed for years to come.

RIVERSIDE
Owned by Bob and Ann Keegan of New York, this kennel was established in 1971 when they obtained their first GSP to be used by Bob as a gundog. In those early years the Keegans were mostly involved in Obedience, and their efforts produced many top-winning Obedience dogs, as well as all-time top Obedience producers.

According to Ann, the turning point for Riverside came in the summer of 1983, when they acquired a nine-month-old bitch, known today as Am. Can. Ch. Cheza's Riverside Imp A/C CD. This bitch was destined to shatter all production records for Show Champions for the breed. 'Samantha' is now the all-time top producing dam of Show Champions, with twenty-five to her credit, and four or five more well on the way to finishing. Further, her get and grand-get are producing well to carry on the tradition.

The Keegans wanted to bring in different lines to blend with their own. As a result, says Ann,

Bob Keegan's Am. and Can. Ch. Cheza's Riverside Imp: This bitch shattered all production records for the breed.

Wm. Gilbert.

there is not one type of 'Riverside' GSP. However, the consistent features in Riverside's production are good temperament, soundness, excellent movement, and nice heads. "One great dog made Riverside a very successful kennel," said Ann.

SERAKRAUT

This kennel originated with the Strauss line, which was an outstanding line bred by the late Del and Val Glodowski. Believing that quality begets quality, some of the fine dogs found in the Serakraut pedigrees today include: Dual Ch. Baron von Strauss, Dual Ch. Hans von Eldridge CD, Dual Ch. Esso von Enzstrand (German imp.), Ch. Strauss's Happy Go Lucky (BIS winner and GSPCA Hall of Fame).

The Serakraut kennel is located on seventy-two acres in Wisconsin, and was established in 1965 when Jim Serak bought his first two GSPs for hunting dogs. Soon Jim's mother, Ann Serak, and his sister, Margie, became involved in showing and breeding the dogs. In 1982 Margie married professional handler Roland Wilson. In almost thirty years the Seraks have bred seventy-eight Champions. These dogs did not just win titles – they distinguished with truly important wins, racking up a total of 107 Specialty wins, including: three National Specialty wins, forty-one Best in Specialty Shows, seventeen Best Opp Sex to Best in Specialty, forty-three Specialty Winners Dog or Bitch, and six Best in Sweepstakes. Additionally, the Seraks' dogs have earned three all-breed Best in Shows, and ten Sporting Group wins.

Serakraut GSPs earn high marks in production also. Happy Go Lucky presently ranks as the third-top show sire of all time, with forty-eight Champions and the top Obedience producing sire

RIGHT: Ann Serak's Ch. Strauss's Happy Go Lucky: Elected to the Hall of Fame in 1990, sire of forty-eight Champions, and twenty-eight Obedience-titled offspring.

E. Frank.

BELOW: Roland and Margie Wilson's Ch. Serakraut's Exactly: The first GSP to win the Sporting Group at the Chicago International.

of all time. Ch. Serakraut's Stardust is the eighth listed all-time producing dam of Show Champions with twelve to her credit, including Best in Show, Group and Specialty winners. An up-and-coming young dog, Ch. Serakraut's Scotch Neat also ranks on the top producer list with fourteen Champions and more promised on the way.

TABOR
Joan and Joel Tabor of New Jersey began showing GSPs in 1976 and their breeding programme started in 1978. Their line is based on Ch. Tabor's Orion CD, a solid liver grandson of the famous Adam v Fuehrerheim, and a descendant of the famous 'Sand' line from Germany, on the dam's side. Orion was a successful show dog and the sire of two National Specialty winners: Ch. Tabor's Zephyr of Orion and Ch. Tabor's Banner of Hidden Acre.

Am. Can. Ch. Tabor's Zephyr of Orion was extensively campaigned in tough East Coast competition, winning more than 135 Best of Breed awards, including a Westminster KC Best of Breed in 1983, multiple Group placements and wins, three all-breed Best in Shows, and four Best in Specialty Shows. To date, Zephyr has produced twenty-five Champions, thirteen Obedience title holders, and four Hunting Test title holders, which place him solidly on the all-time top producer listing for the breed.

Following in the footsteps of their sire and grandsire are Ch. Tabor's Twice as Spicey and Ch. Tabor's Cinnamon Rose CD JH. Each won Futurity classes at the GSPCA National Specialty, in 1981 and 1986 respectively. Spice went on to win Best Opp Sex in Futurity and Sweepstakes at the National. Another Zephyr son, Ch. Tabor's Ladenfield Tuckoma, was Best of Winners at the 1989 Nationals as well as Best Opp Sex in Futurity.

Am. and Can. Ch. Tabor's Zephyr of Orion: National Specialty winner.

Chris and Kenneth Tucker's Ch. Mariah's Marigold: The foundation bitch for the Tuckoma kennel.

TUCKOMA

This kennel started life in 1983, shortly after the marriage of Christine to Kenneth. Chris wanted a breed she could owner/handler to its Championship, as well as having a family pet for their home in New Jersey. Chris and Kenneth have never regretted their choice of the German Shorthaired Pointer, and in the past decade have owned, co-owned, or bred twelve Champions.

Tuckoma's foundation bitch, Ch. Mariah's Marigold, proved to be outstanding in the whelping box. She produced five Champions from only eleven puppies! Four of those have Specialty wins. One of the puppies, Ch. Tuckoma The Wiz, was Chris's first home-bred Champion, a bitch of which she is especially proud. The Wiz wins include Best in Futurity at the National Specialty show, four Specialty show Best in Sweepstakes, a Specialty Best of Breed and Best Opp Sex, and a Group placement. She finished her Championship at 13 months with all wins from Puppy and Bred by Exhibitor classes.

The Wiz is dam to four Champions so far, with more offspring pointed. Her get display all of her fine qualities and have succeeded in the toughest of competition. It would seem that, without doubt, this bitch will some day be one of the breed's top producers.

UP N' ADAM

This kennel was founded by Katrin Higgins Tazza, of Connecticut. To quote her own words: "In studying the pedigrees of outstanding sires, I observed that Ch. Adam von Fuehrerheim and Ch. Gretchenhof Columbia River were produced by out-crossing a line-bred bitch to a dual working dog." Katie decided that this was the route for her line, and patiently worked to that end. She may not have realised, of course, that she was following the same path in principle that hundreds of dog breeders had taken before her!

Katrin Higgins Tazza's Ch. Up N'Adam's Barbara.

Ch. Up N'Adam UD JH: This GSP has won titles in Field, Obedience, and in the show ring.

C.Tatham.

Her foundation bitch, Ch. Up N' Adam's Windsong Mariah CDX was first bred to Ch. Kingswood's Windsong. This produced Ch. Up N' Adam's Barbara CD, and was the groundwork for Katie's outcross to K.S.Zobel vom Pregelufer, the outstanding German import. That breeding, to date, has produced fourteen Champions, one Junior hunter, one Utility Dog, and one Companion Dog Excellent.

Out of these fourteen Champions, eight have wins at Specialty shows, including the 1989 National Specialty Show Sweepstakes winner and 1990 National Specialty Best of Breed winner, Ch. Up N' Adam UD JH. He is the first GSP with titles in breed, field and obedience to win this top award. Nine other get from this breeding are Best of Breed winners, five of them having Group placements. Ch. Up N' Adam has so far produced fifteen Champions, four Junior Hunters, six with wins at Specialty shows and a Sporting Group winner.

Zobel also helped to reinforce the field ability of the Up N' Adam kennel, producing many fine natural gundogs. Two from that breeding have field placements, and the ability is now carried forth in the grand-get. Clearly, the patience and persistence involved in this kennel's breeding programme has resulted in what the German pioneers meant by 'through performance to type'.

WEINLAND
This kennel originated in 1977 in Arizona. Linda Bynum's foundation bitch was Ch. Windsong's Sweet As Candy, an all-time top producer out of two all-time top producers. This bitch was bred three times and produced eleven Champions, including GSPCA Hall of Fame, all-breed Best in Show, National Specialty Best in Futurity, and several top-producing get.

As with most of the best GSP kennels in America, the tradition of excellence continues with the grand-get. At present, Weinland has produced ten litters, twenty-nine Champions, two all-breed Best in Show winners, two National Futurity winners and three all-time top producers.

Linda Bynum's Ch. Windsong's Sweet As Candy: Foundation bitch for the Weinland kennel.

Sue Harrison's Ch. Windsong Misty Memories: Foundation bitch for the Wyndbourne kennel.

Richard Anderson.

WYNDBOURNE

In the summer of 1968 Sue Harrison saw, and fell in love, with a German Shorthaired Pointer at Trapp Family Lodge in Vermont. It was not until four years later that she purchased her first GSP and began showing. The following year she met John Herring of the Windsong kennel at a show, and that meeting resulted eventually in Sue's purchase of Ch. Windsong's Misty Memories, the backbone of Wyndbourne.

Misty finished her Championship in short order with a Best in Sweepstakes and multiple Best of Breed wins. She was campaigned by Sue to many Group wins and placements, and was the 1979 National Specialty Best of Breed winner. Misty proved herself in the whelping box, with eight Show champions, four Obedience titles, and one Junior Hunter to her credit. Her Champion get include two top ten and multiple Group winning bitches, Ch. Wyndbourne's Rembrance and Ch. Wyndbourne's Outrageous, who also won an all-breed Best in Show and six Best in Specialty Shows. Another of her get, Ch. Wyndbourne's Bustin' Loose, is a multiple Group placer and sire of eighteen Champions, with more on the way. Buster is sire of Wyndbourne's second all-breed Best in Show winner, Ch. Wyndbourne's Keepsake.

Despite not breeding more than an average of a litter every two or three years, Wyndbourne has produced twenty-three Champions in nine litters. All the Wyndbourne dogs are proudly breeder/owner handled, and when not in the show ring, they enjoy life at Sue's home in Ft. Lauderdale, Florida.

THE FUTURE

The list of breeders is prodigious: where does one stop? This representative sample of top producing, successful and responsible breeders reflects a healthy state of depth of quality in the breed in the US. There are many other breed names of credit to stand side by side with these few I have listed. Provided those originally accepted principles continue to be upheld, and there is every reason to think that they will be, there can be no doubt about the future of the German Shorthaired Pointer in America. The sense of pride of achievement, so apparent in breeders in the US, is thoroughly justified.

PART II: THE FIELD

INTRODUCTION

Following our visit to the US, we now know many GSP owners, trainers and handlers with similar interests to our own. They include our dear friends, Dianne and Bob Roghair. Both of them have a wealth of experience as competitors and judges in the sport of Field Trials in America. Dianne's involvement with GSPs and trials goes a long way back; she used to go hunting with her father and his two GSPs in the 1940s. Dianne grew up, left home and got her first GSP in 1968. 'Chad' was a smart dog and he had to be – he taught himself, and Dianne learned to train dogs just from hunting with him! Dianne has a competitive nature, and she decided that if she was going to do anything with GSPs it had better be the tops; she had to own and campaign a Dual Champion (most of us are happy to start off hoping for a Certificate of Merit!).

In 1972 she reserved a bitch pup from a 'royally bred' litter. The sire, both granddams and both grandsires were all Duals, and the dam was littermate to another. However, fate took a hand, and Dianne went home with a scruffy little male, next to last pick of a litter of ten! In 1979 that scruffy pup, already Ch. Babes Drifting Toby von Greif also finished as a Field Champion, thus making him the breed's 125th Dual Champion. Dianne never had so much fun or met such great people as she did when she and 'Toby' got into the Field Trial circuits. Win or lose (and they lost as often as they won), Dianne reckons those are the times she will remember when she is confined to a

A hunting party, 1946, with Dianne Roghair's father and grandparents.

LEFT: Ch. Babes Drifting Toby: The breed's 125th Dual Champion.

BELOW: Bob Roghair's Ft. Ch. German Jake von Greif.

rocking chair on the front porch! Dianne and Bob met as Field Trial competitors. His Field Champion German Jake von Greif was a half-brother to Dianne's Toby. Over the years, they bred and finished another eight or nine Champions, campaigned a winner of a US Puppy/Derby, and helped many others prepare their dogs for show and field competition. They have, however, always remained amateur handlers. Dianne and Bob have hunted game across a number of Mid Western States, Minnesota, Iowa, North and South Dakota, Nebraska and parts of Canada. They now live in lovely country just outside the Twin Cities of Minneapolis/Saint Paul, in Minnesota.

TRIALING IN AMERICA

This account of field trialing on the American side of the Atlantic is taken from information provided by Dianne. We have also spent hours talking about GSPs both here and when we stayed as Dianne and Bob's guests during part of our visit to America in 1992. During that stay we also had the great good fortune to meet and talk with George De Gideo, that great GSP Field Trial and show enthusiast. We were able to discuss the merits of trialing and the differences between our systems, during the time we were together. It is not every day that one has the privilege to meet a man who has become a legend in his own lifetime. Dianne has written a short biography of George which I am pleased to include in this chapter.

EARLY TRIALS

In many respects, the early US trials can be closely compared with the current UK system, with all the competitors following the trial on foot or in a wagon, for the whole day. But conditions and time have altered the picture somewhat today. Certain factors have shaped the sport; in fact it is still evolving and may look quite different in the future.

Historically, hunting dogs have been 'tested' any time enthusiastic hunters came together to show off their canine hunting partners. Pointing dog Field Trials originated in the late 1800s and were usually associated with plantation owners. Because their holdings were vast, often amounting to several thousand acres, dogs were hunted and tested from horseback, a practice which continues today in both AKC and the American Field Trials.

Pointers and Setters of those times were released in braces to hunt over a huge tract of land. Interested parties, the 'gallery', would follow the brace on horseback or in a mule-drawn dog wagon until it became their turn to hunt. At the end of the day, the best dog or two were named. As population increased, tracts of land became smaller and Field Trials became a more controlled event, with time limits, rules and specific performance expectations.

When GSPs arrived in the US after World War One, formal field testing began as a foot-handling event, with only the judges and assistant (called the Marshall – equivalent to the UK Chief Steward) mounted. A hunting field was divided by an imaginary centre line and handlers had to stay within a few feet of this line while their dogs hunted to very specific directions and commands.

In the early 1950s, as the GSP became more 'noticeable' as a US Sporting breed, more competitors looked for trials in which to compete. Early competition in Pointer and Setter trials showed (just as it did in the UK) that the GSP and other continental pointing breeds really needed to develop their own Field Trial expectations. Those trials, however, introduced American owners to the look and feel of horseback handling. Today almost all Field Champions have been trained for, and must win, in horseback-handled Field Trial competition.

George De Gideo has a copy of a wonderful old book written by George Ruediger, of Minnesota, in 1953. At that time, the Minnesota GSP Club was the German Shorthaired Pointer Club of

RIGHT: Don Paltani, professional trainer/handler, roading two Field Trial Champions – Stuka of the Knight and Rawhide's Bad News.

BELOW: Don Paltani with six Field Champions: Dixielands Mocha Delight, Stuka of the Knight, Rawhide's Lexington Jake, Rawhide's Bad News, Rawhide's Clown, and Trivial Pursuit.

America. It functioned as such until the mid-1950s, at which time a 'national' club was formed and the Minnesota club became a local member club. George Ruediger founded the Big Island kennel, one of the foundation GSP kennels. That gentleman is long since gone, but the fame of his breeding lives on.

PRESENT-DAY FIELD TRIALS
The Field Trial enthusiast has ample and diverse types of competition in which to test the skills of his or her German Shorthaired Pointer. These range from Field Trials sponsored by local GSP clubs under the regulations of the American Kennel Club, to all-breed trials sponsored by the American Field, and to a variety of natural ability tests organised by groups more tuned to hunting testing than the sport of Field Trials.

AKC LICENSED FIELD TRIALS
The American Kennel Club sponsors hundreds of licensed Field Trials for pointing breeds through its various local breed clubs. For example, the German Shorthaired Pointer Club of Minnesota holds two licensed Field Trials each year. These trials are licensed by the AKC, are run according to AKC rules and regulations, and Championship points are awarded to the stake winners. The title of 'Field Champion' is used by the AKC to complement its 'Champion' (show only) title. A GSP attaining both titles is awarded the rare 'Dual Champion' title.

A typical AKC Field Trial offers both 'Puppy' and 'Derby' juvenile stakes in addition to the following adult stakes: Open Gundog, Amateur Gundog, All-aged, and Limited stakes, the latter reserved for dogs which have previously won or been placed in similar events. At some larger trials, run on multiple courses, it is not uncommon for 110 to 140 dogs to compete; however, most single course trials are run over two weekend days and draw between 65 and 85 entrants. (It is interesting to note here that obviously game-shooting is permitted in the US on Sundays, whereas in the UK it is illegal to shoot game on Sundays and on Christmas Day!)

PUPPY STAKES
Puppies are from 6 to 15 months old, and run 15 minute heats. They are judged on future potential and application to the course. Birds may be encountered, but are not shot, and no extra credit is given for pointing at this age.

DERBY STAKES
Derby dogs are from 6 to 24 months old, and run in 20 minute heats. Derby dogs are judged on future potential, application to the course and bird contact. However, it would seem that more emphasis is placed on covering the course attractively. Birds are released on the course or a bird field and a derby dog is expected to point when making game contact.

The dogs are expected to retrieve if the stake is a retrieving stake, but are not judged especially hard if the retrieve is not polished. A Derby dog is not expected to have a full set of 'manners', and therefore does not receive extra credit for honouring a brace-mate's point or being steady to wing or shot.

ADULT STAKES
Any dog over 6 months can run in an Adult stake. Adult dogs are referred to as 'broke dogs', the slang term for a fully mannered dog. Gundogs and All-aged Dogs are judged on a complete performance that demands superior application to the course, demonstrated ability to locate game

and point stylishly, steadiness to wing (flush) and shot, a retrieve that is prompt and tender to hand, and manners to honour a brace-mate's point.

Both gundogs and all-aged dogs are expected to have a strong, forward-going application that is appropriate to the cover on the course as well as specific to likely bird-holding objectives on the course. A dog that hunts forward in open cover while failing to hunt a forward hedgerow would obviously be penalised.

A dog should handle kindly, with minimal direction from the handler. The all-aged dog hunts independently and takes little direction from the handler. A wider course is acceptable for a gundog, since gundogs are judged under more of a 'hunt to the gun' criterion than all-aged dogs. This subtle distinction can confuse a novice trialer, because hunting to the gun is rather a relative term when running dogs from horseback. Virtually any dog seeing its handler upon a horse will range further afield simply because the handler is easier to see from a distance. Until you establish a comfortable level with the increased range these dogs show, the term 'hunt for the gun' seems inappropriate to some.

An all-aged course runner is supposed to be strong and extremely bold, with an emphasis on independence rather than 'handle'. Many people new to the sport ask why you would want this sort of performance. Dianne's tongue-in-cheek response is: "Like yogurt – it is an acquired taste." The real answer simply lies in how and where you hunt, and in the true vastness of some of the hunting lands in the United States of America.

The rangy performance required for hunting several square miles of Kansas wheat stubble or cattle grazing land would drive an average small farm, or preserve hunting party, quite mad. Likewise, if you have the good fortune to be able to hunt those square miles, but you have a dog without the desire or intelligence to know what to do with all that space, this also makes for an unhappy day. Competing with, and rewarding all-aged dogs ensures that future field dogs have the ground covering skill and independent desire to go, together with native intelligence and training.

CHAMPIONSHIP POINTS AND NATIONAL CHAMPIONS

A GSP must win 10 Championship points to earn either the AKC Field Champion or Amateur Field Champion title. A Field Champion can have won points in either Open stakes or Amateur (handled) stakes. An Amateur Field Champion must earn all points as an amateur handled dog.

The 10 points must be won in a minimum of three separate trials under different judges. Dogs are judged in 'head-to-head' competition, and only the dog judged best in the stake is awarded the blue ribbon and Championship points. The other, not so fortunate competitors congratulate the winner and go home to dream of how it should have been!

Dianne told me that a typical juvenile stake has 15 to 25 entrants; gundog stakes have between 22 and 30, depending on whether the stake is open or amateur, or a limited one. All-age stakes average between 6 and 13 runners at those trials that have the grounds to offer the stake. As it should be, it is difficult to finish an all-aged dog, as opportunities to win major points are few, because many localities do not have the grounds large enough to safely test the dogs. If it were easy, the breed could face a problem of producing mostly dogs that hunt too big for the average hunter – too much spice in the soup!

A stake winner earns from 1 to 5 points depending of the number of dogs defeated in the stake, as follows:

4-7 starters: 1 point.	13-17 starters: 3 points.	25 or more: 5 points.
8-12 starters: 2 points.	18-24 starters: 4 points.	

Joe Miner's Ft.Ch. Buckville's Maggie Mae.

Dierk Davis' Ft.Ch. Rawhide's Clown.

One of the wins must be a major win (3, 4, or 5 points) and 4 of the total 10 points must be earned in shoot-to-kill retrieving stakes (some stakes are non-retrieving or blank pistol stakes if appropriate grounds cannot be located which allow game to be killed). Also, from the 10 points required, a maximum of 2 can be gained from a Puppy stake and 2 from a Derby stake.

The only exception from this general structure is that a dog winning the National Field Trial (all-aged stake) gains the title of 'National Field Champion' of that year. Similarly, a dog winning the National Amateur Field Trial (gundog stake) gains the title of 'National Amateur Field Champion' of that year. This is parallel to the winner of the annual Kennel Club's Championship stake being awarded the title of Field Trial Champion, regardless of previous wins.

A dog winning a Field Champion title and also Champion (show ring) title earns a Dual Champion title. A dog earning an Amateur Field Champion title and also a Champion (show ring), is not given a Dual Champion title, but, as in the UK, retains each title separately. Dianne suggests that this is perhaps because the AKC and the parent GSP Club feel that Open stakes, where you must compete with professional trainers, gives a more prestigious standing to the Dual title.

THE AMERICAN FIELD

The American Field is an old organisation formed primarily for the sport of Field Trials and field competitions for all types of sporting dogs. It offers a separate stud book and registry from the AKC.

AKC trials are loosely based on these older events; however, there are some significant differences. American Field Trials offer juvenile and all-aged stakes, but refer to gundogs as shooting dogs. Local club trials are offered as well as Regional Championships and National events. Thirty-minute heats are run in regular AF trials but one-hour heats are run in all Regional and National Championships. A dog winning a regional stake is referred to as The Regional

Stan Rys' Ft.Ch. Stuka of the Knight.

Martin Wyantt's Ft.Ch. Rawhide's Lexington Jake.

Shooting Dog Champion (or All-aged Champion) for that specific area.

Two GSP organisations are American Field affiliated. They are the National German Shorthaired Pointer Association and the National German Pointing Dog Association (an all-breeds organisation for the German pointing breeds). Both bodies sponsor an annual National Field Trial, and awards a coveted national Championship title to the winner of the national event stakes.

AKC HUNTING TESTS

An alternative to horseback-handled dog trials is becoming quite popular with many GSP enthusiasts. Hunting tests are all foot-handled stakes – only the judges and marshall are mounted for the day's work.

Dogs can compete in three classes: Junior, Senior and Master stakes. In a hunting test dogs are still run in pairs, but are judged to a standard, not compared to each other in 'head-to-head' competition. Hunting Tests are similar to Obedience trials, in that dogs are scored individually and must obtain a qualifying score to win a 'leg' towards a hunting title. Three qualifying scores are required to obtain a Junior Hunter title and four qualifying scores to obtain the Senior or Master Hunter title.

Hunting Test enthusiasts work to ensure judging standards are high, so that a 'better than average' performance is required to qualify. Dogs are judged on a number of criteria: hunting pattern, enthusiastic but controlled application to the course, full attention to the handler's directions when necessary, stylish bird contact and varying degrees of manners depending on the stake.

Junior dogs must find game and point to qualify. Senior dogs must point, retrieve and honour, but are not required to be completely steady. A Master Hunter must exhibit the same degree of steadiness to wing and shot as the broke Field Trial dog. However, Dianne says she believes that in Hunting Tests retrieving is judged more critically than in Field Trials in the US. Hard-mouth certainly will not qualify. An owner attaining a Master Hunter title with his or her GSP can be justifiably proud of owning that rare commodity – a fully trained, attractive going all-purpose hunter.

Hunting Tests are growing in popularity because anyone can compete relatively inexpensively. They do not require access to horses or horseback training grounds, or the expense of hiring a professional trainer. The tests also provide for a reasonable assessment of field ability and a biddable attitude for foot hunting. In fact, some owners of AKC Field Champions compete in these events to demonstrate that a big-going horseback handled dog can handle kindly and intelligently for the foot hunter. The variety of Field Trial types certainly shows the tremendous versatility of our breed, and experienced handlers reckon that the best GSPs know the difference between the different types of work they are asked to do.

GEORGE DE GIDEO

American breed founders set the Dual Champion firmly in their sights as something to be treasured, and many breeders today have that goal as their dream. It matters little which side of the Atlantic we live, our aims are singularly constant.

In the USA a Dual Champion is still something of a rarity. Only one GSP out of about 5,000 pups – one in every 750 litters – earns the title. (Incredibly, I reckon that is about the same in the UK.) To finish and own a Dual Champion is an honour and a tremendous achievement as it means a full Championship in each discipline, both Field and Conformation. To do it twice is almost impossible. To breed and finish four Dual Champions is unheard of – yet George De Gideo of

George De Gideo presenting Nat. Ft.Ch. Desert Dutch, pictured with handler Don Paltani and owner Don Lloyd.

Minneapolis, Minnesota, has done just that! George first achieved fame as a boxer, having 129 amateur and 53 professional bouts, becoming Minnesota Featherweight Champion. He was three years consecutively featherweight Champion in the US Marine Service. While training upper mid-west 'Golden Glove' Champions in 1949, he acquired his first GSP. He is presently President of the GSP Club of Minnesota and his involvement has included trials and shows in most of the states of the US. In forty-odd years George has bred and finished:
Ch. Big Island Vito, Fld. Ch. Big Island Rocco, Ch. De Gideo's Pheasant Lane Franna, Dual Ch. Ritzie, Dual Ch. Rizie's Oranien Rocco, Dual Ch. Rocco's Diamond Kate von Belle, Fld. Ch. Rocco's Big Island Dolly von Greif, Dual Ch. The Flying Dutchman von Rip Traf, Ch. Dutchman's Cinderella von Greif, Ch. Cindy's Wildberg Bo-Jac von Greif and Ch. Bo-Jac's Scooter von Greif.

Carefully planned breeding, a good eye, knowing what he likes in the field, and seeing what complements his dogs has helped George develop this amazing list of Champions – and these are just the dogs he and his wife, Fern, have owned. One of the 'Dutchman's' offspring is National Field Champion Desert Dutch.

George is a tough competitor, but he will always give time to help a newcomer to the game, or to help a friend work out some problem with their dog. Winning is one thing: taking time to help your competitor, knowing he or she might just defeat you next time out, takes a very special person.

SUCCESSFUL BREEDING
There are two American-bred GSPs which illustrate the strength of the breed in the USA – Dual Ch. The Flying Dutchman von Rip Traf, and a son of Dual Ch. Babes Drifting Toby von Greif, Ch. Hocus Pocus. The name of Greif is prominent in both pedigrees, and they go back to a dog considered by many to be the most important single contributor to the breed in the US: the German import, Field Champion Greif Hundscheirmerkogel. Tracing old Greif lines follows two main

paths: the Duals through Yunga to Bride's Brunz von Greif, and the Field Champion side through the von Thalberg line to that famous sire, Fld. Ch. von Thalberg's Fritz II. Later imports through Axel and other field lines crossed successfully with Fritz II produced one of America'a predominant field lines.

On the Dual side, old Greif produced well with Ch. Yunga War Bride – four Duals out of two litters! One of these, Brunz, carried the Dual for another generation, producing three Dual sons, one of which was Oxton's Minado von Brunz. Minado, bred to another Dual, Dolly, produced three Duals: Baron, Baschen and Fagon. Baron in turn produced Dual Ch. Toby and Eva von Keickhefer, while Baschen produced Boss Lady Jodi von Greif, also a National Amateur Field Champion and National Gundog winner. An impressive history indeed!

The numerical strength and standing of the German Shorthaired Pointer in the US today is a testimony both to the charm, temperament, and utilitarian worth of the breed, and to the successful dedication of GSP breeders. Spread, as it is, throughout a vast country, with about sixty breed clubs and well over 150 notable breeding kennels, a personalized review of all those breeders is impractical. My experience of seeing the breed in such record-breaking numbers, and the pleasure of judging so many young German Shorthaired Pointers at Frederick, Maryland, in 1992 has whetted my appetite for more. I look forward eagerly to our next visit to the US to meet more breeders, to see more of their dogs, both in the show ring and in the field.

CANADA

The very varied hunting terrain of Canada lends itself to the use of a utilitarian gundog, and because there are many hunters here who have come to appreciate the other well-documented traits of the GSP, the popularity of the breed here comes as no surprise. Despite the great distances involved (but remembering that the people of the north American continent use air travel in the same way as Londoners use city buses and the underground), there is a great deal of interchange on all sporting levels between the United States of America and Canada. This, of course, includes the dog fancy, and the result is that breeding, and canine competition, overlaps the national border in both directions.

THE SHOW SCENE

Under the guiding control of the Canadian Kennel Club (CKC), dogs of various breeds are grouped together, as in most countries, primarily according to their work-type. The groups are:

Sporting Dogs	Toys
Sporting Dogs (Hounds)	Non-Sporting
Working Dogs	Herding
Terriers	

The German Shorthaired Pointer is included in the Sporting Group with all the other gundog breeds. Championship Shows may be held under license of the CKC for all-breeds or as breed Specialties. The scheduled classes at Championship shows are:

Junior Puppy: For dogs of 6 to 9 months of age.

Senior Puppy: For dogs of 9 to 12 months of age.

The 12 to 18 months class: Self-explanatory, but only available at Specialty shows.

Canadian-bred Class: For dogs born in Canada. All Champions excluded.

Bred by Exhibitor Class: Self-explanatory, but the dog must be handled in the class by the breeder/owner.

Can. Ch. Firefox's Cinder of Ebonyridge CD.

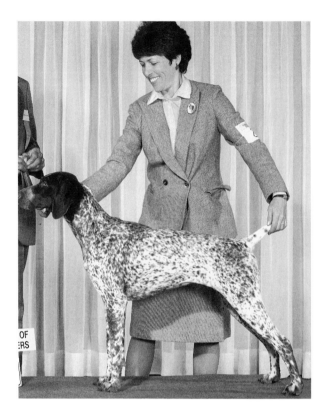

Jerry and Sharon Freeman's Am. Can. Ch. Firefox's Rowdyman Whirlwynd.

Cecilia Delaney's Ch. Sealisle Fame For Rebecca.

Open Class: For all dogs other than Champions.
Veteran Class: For dogs seven years and over. Available only at Specialty shows.
Specials Only Class: For recorded Champions only.

Other non-regular classes may be offered, such as Brace, Team, Stud dog and get, Brood bitch and progeny, and a variety of Sweepstakes Classes. Winners of these classes, other than Specials only, compete for winners dog and/or winners bitch, and these dogs get the points towards Championship status, before going on to contest, with the Specials Only winner, for Best of Breed. Points are awarded to these winners which count towards Championship status. The number of points awarded varies from one to five according to the number of the breed exhibited. In order for a dog to be recognised as a Champion it must have been awarded at least ten points accrued under at least three separate judges, and must be individually registered in the records of The Canadian Kennel Club.

FIELD COMPETITION
Field Trials are held on two levels. A sanctioned Field Trial is an informal trial at which dogs compete, but not for Championship points, sanctioned by the CKC. A licensed Field Trial is a trial at which Championship points may be awarded, which has been specially licensed as such by the CKC. All dogs are run as braces, i.e. dogs are drawn in pairs to run the course together. A dog (or handler) may not interfere with the other dog's work, but must honour its point by 'backing'.

A pointing dog becomes a Field Trial Champion of Record by winning ten points at Field Trials licensed by the CKC. Of the ten points, at least three shall have been won in one unrestricted Senior Open Stake and not more than two points shall have been won in either Puppy or Derby Stakes, but no dog shall be recorded as Field Trial Champion unless it has exhibited the ability to back. Similarly, a dog may become an Amateur Field Trial Champion having won ten points in

Hander/trainer David Clark with OTCh. Cedarpark Imagine AM CD (left) and OTCh. Firefox's Whirlwynd Misty Kate AM CD.

amateur stakes, including a minimum of one three-point win in an Amateur Senior Stake. Any person who receives remuneration or reward for handling or training field trial dogs is by definition classed as a professional handler. All handlers not so classed shall have amateur standing. Dogs running in Amateur Stakes must be owned and handled by an amateur. There are Stakes held for Puppy, Derby dogs, Shooting Dogs and All-aged Dogs. Championship points may be awarded as follows:

Puppy Stakes (5 or more runners) winner:1 point.
Derby Stake (5 to 7 starters) winner: 1 point,
(8 or more starters) winner: 2 points.

All Senior Stakes	First	Second	Third
6 to 7 dogs competing	1	0	0
8 to 11 dogs competing	2	1	0
12 to 15 dogs competing	3	1	1/2
16 to 19 dogs competing	4	2	1
20 or more dogs competing	5	3	2

As in the United States of America, Puppy Stakes and Derby Stakes (respectively for dogs not over 18 months and 27 months of age in Canada) do not call for a polished performance, but look for a dog with nose and drive and the potential ability to be a complete gundog. Shooting and All Aged Dog Stakes call for a polished gundog performance with consideration being given to the following criteria:

OTCh. Extra v.d. Seiger Boss AM CD.

Ch. Chalko's Ceildh of Seal Island.

i. Ground Work – intelligent search, appropriate range, pace.
ii. Bird Work – accurate and quick location and re-location, pointing, style and intensity.
iii. Training and Manners – hunting to the course, responding to the handler, steadiness to wing and shot, retrieving (where required), backing.

In Shoot to Kill Stakes handlers may be required to shoot their own dog's birds. Otherwise, a minimum of two guns are required for each brace. Only free-flying game which has been produced by the dog shall be shot. In Shoot to Kill Stakes the dog will be required to retrieve cleanly and tenderly to hand, one command only, except in Derby Shoot to Kill Stakes where absolute steadiness is not a requirement.

Trials must be run hunting only game normally hunted by pointing dogs in the Province in which the stake is held. The game varieties encountered include Pheasant, Woodcock, Ruff Grouse, Blue Grouse, Quail and Sharptail Grouse.

In Championship Stakes, first series heats must be of not less than 45 minutes duration for each dog. A dog may not be declared a Champion unless it has been shot over when birds are flushed to his point. It is entirely up to the judges to decide whether a winner of the stake shall be declared, and whether there shall be other placements.

The CKC also license Field Dog Tests and Field Dog Excellent Tests – the former for dogs which do not have the title Field Dog, and the latter for dogs which hold the title Field Dog but not Field Dog Excellent. These tests would be similar to a combination of Working Tests and Spring pointing tests as run in the UK. Dogs do not compete with one another but are required to achieve a certain standard of efficiency.

For the purpose of the tests, live game birds may be released or pigeons dizzied and placed in natural cover. Blanks are fired, but no birds are shot. Retrieves are executed on dead birds provided for the purpose.

Field Dog Test scores for perfect performance are:
Desire to hunt: 10 points max.
Style running: 10 points max.
Pace: 10 points max.
Range: 10 points max.
Pattern: 10 points max.
Control: 10 points max.
Pointing: 20 points max.
Reaction to shot: 10 points max.
Retrieve on land: 10 points max.
Maximum total: 100 points.

Field Dog Excellent Test scores for perfect performance are:
Desire to hunt:10 points max.
Style running and pattern: 10 points max.
Range and pace: 10 points max.
Control: 10 points max.
Pointing: 15 points max.
Steady to flush and shot: 15 points max.
Retrieve through water: 10 points max.

Retrieve on land: 10 points max.
Backing: 10 points max.
Maximum Total: 100 points.

In order to gain the official title Field Dog (FD) or Field Dog Excellent (FDX), a dog must:
i. Receive three qualifying scores at three Field Tests.
ii. These three scores to be obtained under at least two different judges.
iii. The dog must be properly registered with CKC.

A qualifying score at these tests is 75 points or more of the possible total of 100, with not less than 50 per cent of the available points for each of the qualities tested. The letters FD or FDX after a dog's registered name denote that the dog has achieved the requirement.

WORKING ORGANISATIONS

There are several organisations apart from breed clubs which cater for the working aspect of the breed. They include The North American Versatile Hunting Dog Association (NAVHDA), which originated in the US and has headquarters at Arlington Heights, Illinois. Prime mover in this association coming into Canada was John Kegal. As well as sponsoring events, a registry is kept and a regular newsletter published. There also exists The National Shoot to Retrieve Association (NSTRA) and The National Bird Hunters Association.

In common with enthusiasts of GSPs in other countries, many Canadian breeders place as much, if not more, emphasis on in-bred work capability as on pure physical merit as assessed in the show ring; and additionally, some owners have had great success in Obedience competition. I have been able to collate some information from an increasing number of kennels where GSPs are bred.

CANADIAN KENNELS

FIREFOX

Owned by Jerry and Sharon Freeman at Mansfield, Ontario, this kennel perhaps typifies the general picture of responsible ownership and breeding seen throughout Canada. Starting out with a GSP bitch in 1980, Jerry and Sharon studied the breed in some depth before eventually successfully breeding Canada's top bitch Champion, Whirlwynd's Winter Edition and producing her litter of six title-holders, some with dual status. Good fortune continued with Am. Can. Ch. Firefox's Rowdyman Whirlwynd, who became one of Canada's top field and show dogs in 1987, at the age of two years. After holding third top spot in the US, 'Rowdy' retired from competition to do the thing he loves best of all, hunting with his master!

Am.Can. Ch. Firefox's A Blazing Whirlwynd became one of Canada's top ten, and his daughter, Ch. Firefox's Cinder of Ebonyridge CD, was top female in Canada. Her litter, not yet two years old, includes three with Championship status and one with a CD title. Sharon says all their dogs are HD, PRA and VWD tested, and their aim, without compromise, is to produce truly all-purpose GSPs, breeding seldom, but with great care and a sense of breed responsibility.

SEALISLE

Formerly Seal Island, this kennel is based at Cape Breton, Nova Scotia, and is owned by Cecilia Delaney. Situated on one hundred acres of field, wood and water, on the Island of Boularderie, Cecilia says this is the perfect setting for GSPs. Her introduction to GSPs was in 1971, and by 1988 she had acquired a bitch, Chalko of Medley. When mated to Am. Can. Ch. Ehrinvogel Song

Sung Blue (the Rugerheim line) she produced two GSP Champions. They were Chalko's Ceilidh of Seal Island CD, and Chalko's Chuckle of Seal Island. A second mating to Leiblinghaus Flagstaff produced Ch. Ringo of Seal Island, No. 3 in the show ring in Canada in 1992. His wins included 61 Best of Breed, and 10 Group firsts.

OBEDIENCE

First at the top in the Obedience field was Tony Butt of Brandon, Manitoba, when, in 1987, Ch. OTCh Rekinil's Sitka became the first GSP to become Canada's top Obedience dog. David and Bonnie Clark, from Gloucester, Ontario, both active members of the GSP Club of Eastern Canada and instructors with the Bytown Dog Obedience Club of Ottawa, have since made up OTCh. Extra v.d. Seiger Boss, bred by Shawn Smith DVM, owned and handled by David. This dog went on to become top GSP, top Sporting Dog and all-time third of all breeds for 1991. Additionally, David and Bonnie have two more GSP Obedience Trial Champions in Cedarpark Imagine Am. CD, and Firefox's Whirlwynd Misty Kate Am. CD. No mean achievement in a highly competitive field.

IMPORTS/EXPORTS

I believe a few UK-bred dogs have been imported into Canada. One at least became Champion. The name of the dog was Eng. Sh. Ch. and Can. Ch. Quarryhall Furry William. Bred by Mrs A. Guimard and owned by Capt. F.G. Noseworthy, the dog was taken back to Canada by the Noseworthys when they returned home after a tour of service duty in the UK. I recall the dog being exhibited in England, but that was nearly twenty years ago. Equally, several Canadian-bred GSPs have come to the UK, One, Can. Ch. Ulda Evan Von Offa was used successfully at stud by both Fio Roberts to Isara Kurzhaar bitches, and by Anne Gill to Birkenwald bitches; the latter producing Show Champions Birkenwald Ilka and Birkenwald Kyra. He also sired Ft. Ch. Chorville Jackson.

Owners and breeders have increased steadily in Canada during the past couple of decades, and the general impression is that the future looks increasingly bright for the GSP in this lovely country.

Chapter Twelve

THE GSP IN BRITAIN

THE SHOOTING SCENE

From the advent of game-shooting as a sport until the outbreak of the 1939-45 war, the pattern of shooting and the use of specialist gundogs to perform the various tasks required of them, was unquestioned in Britain.

Wealthy land-owners employed keepers to rear pheasants and partridges, beaters to produce them to the standing guns, and pickers-up with their dogs to recover the shot birds. Only the Spaniel breeds could have been considered as rough-shooters' dogs, and they were mostly used by keepers and were not expected to hunt wide, nor did they point game. The Retriever breeds performed most of the work, which was, after all, what they were bred for. Pointers, hunting on heather moors for grouse or on wide grain stubbles for partridges, were the real aristocrats of the gundog world, and they were completely specialised, performing purely as game-finding dogs on open ground; never entering cover and not retrieving.

Very few shooting men in Britain had even heard of the utility, all-purpose gundog breeds, for they were, when all was said and done, superfluous to their needs. But the war and its aftermath brought about many changes. By and large, the remnants of the old feudal system were swept away, many large country estates were divided, broken up, sold off – and a new breed of sportsmen emerged. Shooting on a much smaller scale became the vogue, and that opened the door for the all-purpose gundog, headed by the German Shorthaired Pointer.

THE FIRST IMPORTS

It fell to officers in the army of occupation and to members of the Control Commission to discover, during their sojourn in Germany, the delights of shooting over a dog which could 'do it all'; and sure enough, a very few of them, probably no more than a dozen, brought Shorthairs back home with them to form the initial breeding stock in the UK. There were two initial drawbacks. Firstly, the breed carried the name 'German', not an entirely popular word in England immediately after five years of bitter warfare. Secondly, although the enthusiasts who were the early importers may have been experienced shooting men, few, if any of them, were knowledgeable dog breeders.

The result was that some of the dogs they brought into Britain, though maybe exciting to shoot over, were not very suitable as breeding stock; nor did the early importers have any experience or expertise in breeding from what they had. Nevertheless, a few of the early imports did carry good blood, and as the popularity of the breed began to increase, more experienced people adopted it, and in due course, some very good dogs were produced from a tiny gene pool. Slowly the GSP was slotted into the sporting scene of Great Britain, and today, whilst its numbers are still only small compared with the Retriever and Spaniel breeds, it holds an accepted place in the field, and its virtues are being appreciated by ever-increasing numbers of sportsmen.

The fact that only a small gene pool was available tended to concentrate the type, and although there have been several imports since those early days, there has not been the very wide choice of blood available in the UK as there has in other countries. It is a generally acknowledged fact that the British are held in high regard as breeders of good pedigree dogs – which may be contributory to the fact that GSPs are now frequently listed amongst our canine exports.

REGISTRATIONS

Today there are some 10,000 GSPs registered with the Kennel Club. Perhaps only ten per cent are exhibited, and fewer still are run in field trials, but many are the beloved shooting companions of men who get immense pleasure from owning, training and shooting over this remarkable breed of utility gundog.

The great bonus, which is to the benefit of GSP owners in Britain, is that there is no divergence of type between the show/companion dog and the worker/field trialer: there is only one German Shorthaired Pointer type in the UK. Not all are used as hunting dogs, not all are exhibited. Indeed, not all would perform creditably in both these activities, but they could do so. This is unlike the Retriever and Spaniel breeds, even the Pointers and Setters, where quite a different type has evolved in the field from that in the show ring.

THE SHOW SCENE

In relation to the size of Britain, the show scene is on a big scale. There are over thirty all-breed Championship Shows annually, plus two breed Specialty Shows at which the GSP enthusiast can exhibit. Only Kennel Club registered dogs can be entered at these shows. The most prestigious of all is Crufts Dog Show, organised and controlled by the Kennel Club. It is the big event of the year, and only dogs which have obtained certain high awards at the previous year's shows may compete. A few pretty ordinary specimens do, oddly enough, get the necessary award, but mostly the entrants are the best representatives of their breed in the country.

There is usually a total of 10,000 to 14,000 dogs of all breeds at the average Championship Show and about 22,000 at Crufts, of which between 100 and 300 are GSPs. Most shows last two, three, or four days, depending on the size of the venue and almost all of them are benched. All gundogs will be judged on one day, and the final Gundog Group winner will be required to come back on the last day to contest for Best in Show.

DIVISION OF CLASSES

At Championship level, each breed is judged separately in a selection from the following complete list of approved classes:

Minor Puppy: 6-9 months of age.

Puppy: 6-12 months of age.

Junior: 6-18 months of age.

Beginners: for owner, handler or exhibit not having won a First Prize at a Championship Show.

Maiden: for dogs which have not won a Challenge Certificate or a First Prize at an Open or Championship Show (puppy classes excepted).

Novice: for dogs which have not won a Challenge Certificate or three or more First Prizes at Open or Championship Shows (puppy classes excepted).

Tyro: for dogs which have not won a Challenge Certificate or five or more First Prizes at Open or

Championship Shows (puppy classes excepted).
Debutant: for dogs which have not won a Challenge Certificate or a First Prize at a Championship Show (puppy classes excepted).
Undergraduate: for dogs which have not won a Challenge Certificate or three or more First Prizes at a Championship show (puppy classes excepted).
Graduate: for dogs which have not won a Challenge Certificate or four or more First Prizes at a Championship Show (puppy classes excepted).
Post Graduate: for dogs which have not won a Challenge Certificate or five or more First Prizes at a Championship show in Minor Limit, Mid Limit, Limit or Open classes.
Minor Limit: for dogs which have not won two Challenge Certificates or three or more First Prizes at Championship Shows in Minor Limit, Mid Limit, Limit, or Open Classes confined to the breed, where Challenge Certificates were offered for the breed.
Mid Limit: for dogs which have not won three Challenge Certificates or five or more First Prizes at Championship Shows in Mid Limit, Limit or Open classes.
Limit: for dogs which have not won three Challenge Certificates under three separate judges or seven or more First Prizes at Championship Shows in Limit and Open Classes confined to the breed at shows where Challenge Certificates were offered for the breed.
Open: for all dogs of the breed for which the class is provided.
Veteran: for dogs over seven years of age on the first day of the show.
Champion: (a rare special class) for dogs which have been confirmed as Champion, Show Champion or Field Trial Champion.

Reproduced by permission of the Kennel Club (classes for multiples, i.e. Brace, Team, etc., are not included).

CC WINNERS
Generally, these classes are split separately for dogs and bitches and there are commonly six or seven classes for each sex at a show, selected from the above list, but always including Puppy, Junior, Limit and Open at least. The winners of each of the classes can be called by the judge after the classes are completed to compete for Best Bitch and Best Dog. Each of these has the opportunity to gain a Challenge Certificate but the granting of it is not automatic.

The prizes are awarded by the show organisers, but the CCs at all shows are awarded by the Kennel Club. Judges, who also have to be approved by the KC, are particularly asked to award the CC only if they are satisfied that the specimen is of such outstanding merit as to be worthy of the title of Champion. A statement to that effect is on the certificate which is signed by the judge.

The best of each sex then compete for Best of Breed. In due course, the Best of Breed of each of the Gundogs compete for Best in the Gundog Group (as do the breeds in the other groups), and the grand finale of the show reaches its climax when the six group winners, i.e. the best one from each of the groups for Gundogs, Hounds, Terriers, Utility, Toys and Working, come together to contest the top spot of Best in Show. Under British rules there is no other CC winning class. All the aspirants to the title have to compete with the existing Champions, who compete in the Open class, so a CC can only be awarded to a dog which is already a Champion or has, on that day, beaten all the Champions entered.

BECOMING A CHAMPION
In order to gain the title of Champion, a dog must win three CCs under three different judges, at

least one of which must be gained after the dog is twelve months old. This method of making dogs up to Champion is a good one, in that it ensures the maintenance of a high standard for the title. Only the 'best' dog can get there. In some other countries, aspirants to the title do not have to beat the existing Champions, which allows a 'second best' dog to get its title and so may lower the standard. Conversely, many a good dog in the UK is denied its title because it is 'held back' by existing Champions. Maybe the system applied in any one country is the best for the dogs and owners of that country – presumably their canine administrators think so!

CHAMPIONSHIP TITLES
These apply to all gundogs, and therefore to GSPs.
Show Champion: A dog which has won three CCs, as above.
Champion: A Show Champion which has also proved its ability as a working dog by winning a field trial award, or at least a Show Gundog Working Certificate.
Field Trial Champion: A dog which has won two Open Qualifying Field Trial Stakes.
Champion and Field Trial Champion: A dog which is a Champion in the field and in the show ring. This is commonly referred to as a 'dual' Champion, but the term is incorrect. There is no such official title granted by The Kennel Club.

CHAMPIONSHIP STATUS
Since Championship status was granted to GSPs some forty years ago there have been many Champions. A very few have attained the title Champion and Field Trial Champion; there have been rather more Field Trial Champions, considerably more Champions and an overall majority of Show Champions. However, something over forty per cent of all titled GSPs in Britain have held field awards, and that is a tremendous achievement compared with all the other gundog breeds.

Interestingly, the majority of the Champions have also been produced from a relatively small number of breeders. Looking at their breeding we see that most of the influential blood is from strong bitch lines. It could be argued that the male line of inheritance is the dominant one, as is accepted in human society. But in dogdom the selective process is different. The breeding policies are determined primarily by the owners of bitches; they decide which males shall be mated to their females. The strength of a pedigree therefore lies in the bitch line through each generation.

When you are looking at a pedigree, you should first consider the strength of the direct bitch line. Owners of not-so-good bitches frequently use the services of the top winning sires. Such matings do not always produce top-quality puppies. However, you can be reasonably sure that the breeder of a top winning bitch will not use an inferior dog as a sire. The breeder may not always use a Champion. The aim is to strengthen or improve the bloodline by using a dog whose blood complements that of the bitch, rather than merely put another red name (Champion) on the pedigree. It is essentially desirable to attach importance to working ability in a gundog breed, and so greater credence is given to a Champion where the title is work-associated; but even more so when it is work and beauty combined. The 'cream' of the titled dogs are the so-called 'duals'. The title is extremely rare in Britain. In GSPs there have only been eight in the past forty-three years, but in all the other breeds of gundog there has not been a single one. Not a Pointer or a Setter, not a Spaniel or a Retriever, not even another HPR breed, has attained the dual title in that time. If you look at the American story, you see a different pattern, but a different system is applied too.

Next in line comes the dogs with the title 'Champion'. They have proven ability in both the field and the show ring, though they are not so successful in the field as the 'duals'. Third are the Field Trial Champions, excelling in the field but untested for conformation. Such dogs can be a danger to the breed if we are to maintain a high standard of combined work and conformational quality. Field Trial Champion dogs can be slightly sub-standard specimens; maybe not good enough in conformation to be used for breeding. The system which is applied in Germany, which requires Field Trial winners to have at least an agreed standard of physical quality, would rectify this. The horrendous schism which now exists between Retriever and Spaniel types of working and show dogs in the UK, was undoubtedly partly due to enthusiastic shooting men not being concerned with the physical correctness of what they bred. Their dogma was not 'through performance to type', but 'through performance to performance', completely ignoring physical type.

Finally, there are the Show Champions – dogs which succeed in the show ring but are not tested in the field. Here lies the opposite danger – that we eventually have a lovely breed of dog with the work potential bred out because of non-usage. It has been stated that dogs bred but not worked through six generations lose their inherited instincts. Could this happen to our breed? Well, of course it could if no one takes steps to avoid it. Admittedly, for one reason or another, there are examples of Champions from good working stock which do not make good in the field. But, unfortunately, the main reason why dogs which win in the show ring are not worked, is that the owners do nothing about the work potential of their dogs. This could be because they are not in a position to be active in the field, but it also because they do not care to do so.

If you are interested in the future of the breed, and you are keen to follow the aspirations of the early pioneers, the title of Show Champion has little value, unless it can be shown that the individual animal can work, although not proven in Field Trials. There are those who think differently, even to the point of supporting anti-blood sports campaigns. This is a matter of personal preference if you are keeping a companion dog, but it is highly debatable whether a breeder of hunting gundogs can legitimately hold such a view. It is impossible to ignore the obvious fact that German Shorthaired Pointers were in the past, are now, and will be in the future, bred to be hunting, game-finding dogs to enhance the sport of hunting and shooting game. Long may that continue!

FIELD TRIALS
Field Trials for gundogs have been held in Great Britain for well over a hundred years. The trials are organised for the specialised groups of gundogs, and until after the 1939-45 War they were only for Pointers and Setters, Retrievers, and Spaniels. Naturally, the trials have to be different for each group as their work schedule is different. The object of Field Trials is two-fold. Firstly, the aim is for owners/breeders to see (by competition) which are the best performing dogs, and to plan their breeding programmes accordingly; and secondly the trials are staged for the enjoyment of competition between like-minded sportsmen. The earliest German Shorthaired Pointer trialers were allowed only to run in Pointer and Setter trials, as there was no group for 'Utility' gundogs in the UK system. They had some success running against Pointers and Setters, although the full role of the GSP – including hunting cover and retrieving – was not tested, as the trials only tested the game-finding capability of the dogs. In 1958, mainly at the request of the GSP Club and its members, the KC established a group for dogs which hunt, point and retrieve, and after much discussion it was called just that, The Hunt Point and Retrieve Group, and since then it has always been referred to as the HPR Group in both show ring and field.

So for the first time in the UK it was possible for GSPs to be tested in their complete role when competing in the field. Not many dogs ran in these early trials, but they were all owned by ardent shooting men and the standard of work was high. Judges for these trials were appointed from the few experienced owners and from the Pointer and Setter judges list. With the development of the breed, Field Trial activities have increased accordingly and today there are some sixty stakes a year held in the UK, licensed by the KC, for the HPR group, and there is a goodly list of competent judges who have come 'up through the ranks' during the past thirty-five years.

FIELD TRIAL REGULATIONS
Trials in the UK are run under the regulations and rules imposed by the KC. There are rules of organisation applicable to all the gundog groups, but those applying solely to the HPR group are reproduced below, by kind permission of the Kennel Club.

BREEDS WHICH HUNT, POINT AND RETRIEVE.
a. Basic Requirements: Dogs shall be required to quarter ground in search of game, to point game, to flush on command, to be steady to flush, shot and fall, and to retrieve tenderly on command from land or water.
b. Number of Runners: With the exception of The Hunt, Point and Retrieve Championship, the maximum number of runners in stakes is as follows – One-day Stake: 12; Two-day Stake: 18.
c. Competing: Dogs shall be run singly in order of the draw under two judges judging as a pair. A dog must have been tried at least twice in the line, excluding the water retrieve, before it may receive an award.
d. Eliminating Faults: Hard mouth – whining or barking – flushing up wind – out of control – running in or chasing – failure to hunt or point – missing game birds on the beat – refusal to retrieve or swim.
e. Major Faults: Not making good ground – missing game on the beat – unsteadiness – sticking on point – persistent false pointing – not acknowledging game going away – failing to find dead or wounded game – catching unwounded game – disturbing ground – noisy handling – changing game whilst retrieving.

SPRING POINTING TESTS
In England, in Europe, and I suspect elsewhere, there is a period of time when partridges are paired but have not commenced nesting. This coincides with the winter-sown wheat having grown just high enough to offer cover to the birds, but not having reached the height where walking over it would cause any damage. This two or three week period is when Spring Pointing Tests can be held. Generally, the object is to run dogs on open ground to test the natural ability of the dog to hunt, point and hold partridges.

It is possible to run the same type of event on a grouse moor, immediately before the shooting season opens, hunting and pointing coveys of young grouse. Absolute steadiness, not being an inherited trait, is not essential, providing the dog does not run amok. Game is not shot.

These tests are not competitive, one dog against another. Dogs are judged individually on the standard of their work. Accordingly a dog may be graded, 'Excellent', 'Very Good' or 'Good'. There are no other grades. The tests are most enjoyable and are viable as assessment opportunities for young dogs particularly. Because they are not competitive, Spring Pointing Tests do not come under the jurisdiction of the KC; but, by general agreement, the judges chosen are always members of the KC senior judges list.

WORKING TESTS
The KC does have some control over working tests, but only to the extent of ensuring that they do not get out of hand or become unrealistic. Virtually all the HPR clubs hold these tests in the Spring

and Summer. The day consists of several individual events designed to test the working capability of gundogs. No game is shot, though 'cold game' is sometimes used for retrieving instead of dummies. Caged birds are often 'planted' for pointing tests. Occasionally, due to the over-enthusiasm of the organisers, the tests display a lack of realism: they should be restricted to situations which can be expected to occur on a shooting day.

These activities are good fun, affording the opportunity for social intercourse as well as offering the chance to test the capability of your trainee dog. There are separately set tests for 'Puppy','Novice' and 'Open'. The tests are usually advertised in the HPR breed societies magazines and newsletters. Spectators are welcome at these events, providing they do not disrupt the proceedings.

THE ROLE OF THE KENNEL CLUB
The Kennel Club plays a very important role in the control of canine activities. It registers all pure-bred dogs and records their pedigrees. It issues regulations and rules which control all canine affairs (excepting working hounds), and approves judges whom it considers capable and honest to adjudicate at all competitive activities. It is the body which owns and is responsible for the organisation of Crufts, the largest dog show in the world. The KC also has close liaison with most of the other canine controlling bodies throughout the world. The establishment of breed clubs (in the case of GSPs, The German Shorthaired Pointer Club and The German Shorthaired Pointer Association) is also licensed and controlled by the KC.

THE BREED SOCIETIES
The German Shorthaired Pointer Club, founded by those few early stalwarts, was formed under the presidency of Geoffrey Sterne, whose strong hand held the wheel until his death only a few years ago. The officials of the club, working with the KC, saw official recognition for the breed and establishment of the group with its own Field Trials and the breed's individual Championship status. Virtually all the other breed clubs of the HPR group have followed in the footsteps made by the early GSP enthusiasts. The foundation they laid has proved a valuable legacy from which all have benefited.

With the approbation of the KC, The GSP Association came into being almost twenty years later. Broadly speaking, there is no conflict and the two societies run happily side by side. Two clubs afford the opportunity for more trials (each runs between fifteen and twenty stakes a year), more shows (each has its own Championship Show annually), and there is the opportunity for inter-club competition. The present membership of each body is between six and eight hundred. No doubt many owners are members and supporters of both Club and Association, and there is every reason why they should be.

There is also a group society known as The Field Trial Association for Hunt, Point and Retrieve Breeds. It has no members, other than two representatives from each of the HPR Field Trial organising breed societies, and one representative from each of the non-breed-specialist clubs which also hold HPR trials. Its objective is to form a forum for the consideration of all field trial matters of interest to the HPR group, advising the associated clubs accordingly, and to represent that group to the KC. It has also taken on the organisation of the annual Championship Stake, which it does on behalf of the KC, as well as holding judges seminars and tuition days.

BREED INFLUENCES
Some fifteen years ago, it was relatively easy to know practically every individual show and Field

*David Atkinson's Ch.
Nevern Jasper – at 15
months.*

*Jane Farrand's (now
Cule) dog, Ch.
Larberry Link.*

A. Roslin Williams.

Trial GSP in the country, and to research a list of the Champions, and their history was well within an author's capability and the limitations of the size of a book. This is not the case today. The following section is therefore devoted to those dogs and their breeders considered to have had the greatest influence on the breed in the UK.

INFLUENTIAL GSPS
The following is not intended to be a complete record of UK Champions. It certainly is not that; but it does show that a great majority of the UK top dogs come from that small pool of leading bloodlines. Some explanation of the apparent maze of registered names may help to clarify the situation. In the UK registration regulations were less strict fifty years ago than they are now. You could then sell an unregistered puppy to a purchaser, who could then register it with his or her own prefix. Looking at records today, this is sometimes confusing. Later the regulations were tightened, and at present only the breeder of a puppy may register it.

Therefore a theoretical 'Inchmarlo Boyo' must have been bred by Mr I.E.T.Sladden, who owns that prefix. The dog may then be purchased perhaps by Mrs M.A.Layton, who can then re-register

Patrick and Mary Godby's Ch. Weedonbrook Elizabeth and Weedonbrook Wanda.

an alteration of the name, but only to add her own prefix to the existing registered name; so the puppy could become 'Inchmarlo Boyo of Midlander'. This addition may only be made once to any dog, and the addition must only be added at the end of the name. By looking at a dog's registered name, therefore, you will know who the breeder was, and who was the subsequent owner, providing they both have registered prefixes. No matter how many times the dog may change ownership, the name cannot be altered again.

NEVERN

Initially, breeding in the UK was restricted, as very few animals were available as producers. The first real prefix to emerge was Nevern, owned by Mr and Mrs Wilfred Simpson. From the imported sire, Saltus von der Forst Brickwedde, carrying the name of a leading German bloodline, came some Champions of note and achievement. They include:

Ch. Nevern Jasper (Saltus v d Forst Brickwedde – Nevern Jenny)
Ch. Nevern Jagd Magdchen (Saltus v d Forst Brickwedde – Nevern Jenny)
Ch. Everserve Rolf (Claus of Cellerhof – Nevern Jagd Magdchen)
Ch. Springfarm Sandpiper (Ch. Nevern Jasper – Nicola of Stockhill)
Ch. Sparrowswick Weiss Jaeger (Saltus v d Forst Brickwedde – Everserve Erica)
Ft. Ch. Littlestat Salamander of Cellerhof (Ch. Nevern Jasper – Octava)
Ch. Ferrier Jaeger (Saltus v d Forst Brickwedde – Bramble of Windlehill)
Ft. Ch. Littlestat Susie (Ch. Nevern Jasper – Octava)
Ch. Littlestat Condiment (Ch. Nevern Jasper – Octava)
Sh. Ch. Larberry Fern (Ch. Nevern Jasper –Weedonbrook Wunder)
Ch. Mordax Morning Mist (Ch. Nevern Jasper – Weedonbrook Wunder)
Ch. Larberry Link (Ch. Nevern Jasper – Weedonbrook Wunder).

*Joyce Robert's
Ch. Midlander
Sirius.
H. Fisher.*

*Sh.Ch.
Midlander
Carina.

Pearce.*

In parallel, from the imported bitch Ch. Weedonbrook Elizabeth, Mary Godby and Jean Rawson bred the bitches Weedonbrook Wunder, Ch. Dunpender Weedonbrook Werra and Ch. Brownridge Marga. From the imported dog Isgo von Blitzdorf, owned by Mrs E. de Havilland, came the 'Roman Numerals' litter containing Sh. Ch. Decima and Octava, which latter so influenced Ch. Nevern Jasper's production.

The general picture in the beginning, therefore, showed that most of the good influence was from dominant sires mated to a variety of bitches. Octava and Ch. Weedonbrook Elizabeth were particularly important dams.

MIDLANDER

Ch. Brownridge Marga was the foundation bitch of the Midlander GSPs, owned and bred by my wife, Mic Layton. It is of some interest that every Midlander pedigree goes back on a direct bitch line to Marga, and therefore to Ch. Weedonbrook Elizabeth. Mic used a number of different sires, in-breeding to Ch. Larberry Link; line-breeding with established Midlanders and out-crossing to Inchmarlo, Appeline and the American import, Adams Hagen von Waldenburg. This dog came from California through UK quarantine, and did his six months mandatory residence here with us. He arrived as an American Champion, and gained his show title here before going out to Georgina Byrne in Western Australia, where he also attained title. He mated only four carefully selected bitches in England and produced several Champions from them. He had just about the best hindquarter action I have ever seen, and passed it on to some of his progeny. He has now been accepted in the American GSP Hall of Fame. Midlander has produced the following Champions:

Ch. Midlander Eider (Ch. Larberry Link – Ch. Brownridge Marga) – this was Marga's only Midlander litter.

Ch. Midlander Mark Antony (Sh. Ch. Appeline Chough – Ch. Midlander Eider)

Sh. Ch. Midlander Moonstone (Ch. Larberry Link – Ch. Midlander Eider)

Ch. Midlander Marcasite (Ch. Larberry Link – Ch. Midlander Eider)

Sh. Ch. Midlander Carina and Ch. Midlander Sirius (both by Ch. and Ft. Ch. Inchmarlo Graff Greiff of Praha – Ch. Midlander Eider)

Ch. Midlander Sioux (Ch. Larberry Link – Ch. Midlander Eider)

Sh. Ch. Firhouse Midlander Rinda (Sh. Ch. Appeline Chough – Midlander Shawnee)

Ch. Midlander Peer Gynt (Ch. Midlander Mark Antony – Midlander Capella)

Sh. Ch. Midlander Chenin (Ch. Midlander Sirius – Midlander Oriental Ranee)

Ch. Midlander Sumatra (Inchmarlo Ballyragget – Midlander Oriental Ranee)

Ch. Midlander Musigny and Sh. Ch. Midlander Monthelie (both by Inchmarlo Ballyragget – Midlander Mistral)

Sh. Ch. Midlander The 'cisco Kid (Sh. Ch. Am. Ch. and Aust. Ch. Adams Hagen von Waldenburg – Midlander Oriental Ranee)

Ch. Midlander Mingan (Ch. Midlander Sumatra – Midlander Mistral)

Sh. Ch. Midlander Sestertius at Vaternish (Sh. Ch. Midlander The 'Cisco Kid – Ch. Midlander Musigny)

Sh. Ch. Midlander Mi Mudle (Ch. and Ft. Ch. Stairfoot Sobrig – Ch. Midlander Mingan).

FIRHOUSE

Based on their foundation bitch, Sh. Ch. Firhouse Midlander Rinda, Margaret and Howard Fisher, bred: Ch. Firhouse Tarka, Sh. Ch. Firhouse Fiery Copper, Ch. Firhouse Mountain Ringlet, and Ch. Firhouse Marbled White, all by Ch. Midlander Sirius out of Sh. Ch. Firhouse Midlander Rinda;

they also produced Sh. Ch. Firhouse Scabious (Sh. Ch. Inchmarlo Fodhla – Sh. Ch. Firhouse Tarka).

SWANSCOE
In turn, Ch. Firhouse Marbled White was the foundation bitch of Elizabeth Ashton's Swanscoe prefix, which produced: Sh. Ch. Swanscoe Spellbinder and Ch. Swanscoe Slightly Seductif, both by Ch. Inchmarlo Deutschmark out of Ch. Firhouse Marbled White, and Ch. Swanscoe Surely Suggestif (Ch. Midlander Sumatra – Ch. Swanscoe Slightly Seductif).

LINKLANDER
Elsewhere, under the ownership of Audrey Ashforth, the prefix Linklander based on Ch. Midlander Marcasite, produced: Sh. Ch. Linklander Caspian, Sh. Ch. Linklander Lippizzaner, and Sh. Ch. Linklander Juniper, all by Sh. Ch. Appeline Chough out of Ch. Midlander Marcasite.

Additionally, Midlander, Firhouse, Swanscoe or Linklander was the prefix of either the sire (S) or the dam (D) of each of the following Champions:
Sh. Ch. Tannahill Weaver of Bryburn (S) Sh. Ch. Firhouse Fiery Copper.
Sh. Ch. Hillanhi Hjordis (S) Ch. Midlander Peer Gynt.
Ft. Ch. Heathlander Lindisfarne (D) Linklander Celandine.
Ch. Inchmarlo Solas (S) Ch. Midlander Sirius.
Sh. Ch. Inchmarlo Deutschmark (S) Midlander Tarku.
Ft. Ch. Wishtonwish Samson (D) Midlander Ursa.
Sh. Ch. Quaxpond Cadence (D) Midlander Calpurnia.

Eric Wheeler's Ft. Ch. Wishtonwish Samson, in turn, sired: Sh. Ch. Rebellious Barbarian, Ft. Ch. Hurlston Wheelwood Commander, Ch. Quintana Tyr and Ft. Ch. Kentoo Pollyanna.

DUNPENDER
Ch. Weedonbrook Elizabeth was also the dam of Ch. Dunpender Weedonbrook Werra, foundation bitch of Michael Brander's famous and important bloodline, carrying the prefix Dunpender. From this prefix the foundation GSPs to New Zealand and Australia were exported. From Ch. Dunpender Weedonbrook Werra came:
Ch. Dunpender Brian (Held of Primrose Bay – Dunpender Fredricka)
Ft. Ch. Dunpender Kate (Hector of Eshtop – Dunpender Impala.)
Ft. Ch. Inchmarlo Heidi (Brechan Hellier – Dunpender Caroline).
A Dunpender GSP was also either sire or dam of:
Sh. Ch. Inchmarlo Elsa (S) Dunpender Duncan (D) Dunpender Constance.
Sh. Ch. Patrick of Malahide (S) Ch. Dunpender Brian.

INCHMARLO
Ian Sladden's very famous and successful Inchmarlo prefix has given its name to a myriad of stars. Unlike Midlander, which all stemmed from the same bloodstock of Ch. Brownridge Marga, Inchmarlo has had several diversified base breeding bitches, the product of which have been successfully inter-bred to create the Inchmarlo family. The list of Champions is prodigious:
Ft. Ch. Inchmarlo Heidi (Brechan Hellier – Dunpender Caroline)
Ch. and Ft. Ch. Inchmarlo Graff Greiff of Praha (Fritz of Praha – Deanslane Daystar of Praha – from Ireland)
Sh. Ch. Inchmarlo Elsa (Ch. Dunpender Duncan – Dunpender Constance)

Ch. Inchmarlo Dunkeld and Ch. Inchmarlo Cora both by Ch. and Ft. Ch. Inchmarlo Graff Greiff of Praha out of Inchmarlo Tamara
Ch. Inchmarlo Raphoe (Karl – Ch. Inchmarlo Cora)
Ft. Ch. Inchmarlo Tuscan (Ch. and Ft. Ch. Inchmarlo Graff Greiff of Praha – Ft. Ch. Inchmarlo Heidi)
Sh. Ch. Inchmarlo Deutschmark (Midlander Tarku – Imme von der Saarner Mark – Imp.)
Ch. Inchmarlo Solas (Ch. Midlander Sirius – Inchmarlo Khamsin)
Sh. Ch. Inchmarlo Coramor (Sh. Ch. Inchmarlo Deutschmark – Ch. Inchmarlo Cora)
Sh. Ch. Inchmarlo Fodhla (Inchmarlo Ballyragget – Inchmarlo Markee)
Sh. Ch. Inchmarlo Camus O May (Sh. Ch. Inchmarlo Deutschmark – Ch. Inchmarlo Raphoe)
Sh. Ch. Inchmarlo Felix (Sh. Ch. Inchmarlo Coramor – Inchmarlo Markee)
Sh. Ch. Inchmarlo Carolina and Sh. Ch. Inchmarlo Montana both by Sh. Ch. Am. Ch. and Aust. Ch. Adams Hagen von Waldenburg out of Sh. Ch. Inchmarlo Camus O May
Sh. Ch. Inchmarlo Ragot Mai (Sh. Ch. Inchmarlo Felix – Sh. Ch. Inchmarlo Carolina).

Individual Inchmarlo sires and/or dams were responsible for the following:
Ch. Midlander Sirius (S) Ch. Ft. Ch. Inchmarlo Graff Greiff of Praha.
Sh. Ch. Midlander Carina (S) Ch.Ft. Ch. Inchmarlo Graff Greiff of Praha.
Sh. Ch. and Can. Ch. Quarryhall Furry William (D) Inchmarlo Inchegeelag.
Ch. and Ft. Ch. Mathams Dark Claret of Trolanda (D) Inchmarlo Dark Damsel.
Ch. McLuskie of Quassingburgh (S) Ch. Inchmarlo Dunkeld.
Ch. Seekon Alex (D) Inchmarlo Marka.
Ft. Ch. Mathams Goshawk (D) Inchmarlo Dark Damsel.
Ch. and Ft. Ch. Swifthouse Tufty (D) Inchmarlo Donenji.
Ch. Midlander Sumatra (S) Inchmarlo Ballyragget.
Sh. Ch. Seekon Son of Brook of Bryburn (D) Inchmarlo Marka.
Sh. Ch. Monttaber Atlantic (S) Inchmarlo Ballyragget.
Ch. Midlander Musigny (S) Inchmarlo Ballyragget.
Sh. Ch. Swanscoe Spellbinder (S) Sh. Ch. Inchmarlo Deutschmark.
Ch. Swanscoe Slightly Seductif (S) Sh. Ch. Inchmarlo Deutschmark.
Sh. Ch. Firhouse Scabious (S) Sh. Ch. Inchmarlo Fodhla.
Ch. Lochpointer Benje (S) Sh. Ch. Inchmarlo Fodhla.
Ft. Ch. Coburn Olivia (S) Inchmarlo Gur.
Sh. Ch. Midlander Monthelie (S) Inchmarlo Ballyragget.
Sh. Ch. Ardenside Gandalf (S) Inchmarlo Bix (D) Inchmarlo Coraneen.
Ch. Shaleward Mustella (S) Sh. Ch. Inchmarlo Coramor.
Ch. and Ft. Ch. Stairfoot Sobrig (S) Sh. Ch. Inchmarlo Fodhla.
Sh. Ch. Stormridge Midnight (S) Sh. Ch. Inchmarlo Montana.
Sh. Ch. Barleyarch Panther (S) Sh. Ch. Inchmarlo Montana.
Ft. Ch. Kentoo Pollyanna (D) Inchmarlo Bibi.

WITTEKIND

Wittekind has been the very successful prefix of a Dutch-born lady, Mineke Mills de Hoog, who has devoted much of her life to breeding GSPs. After the quite recent death of her husband, she has now moved to live in France and has taken numerous dogs with her. Her production of GSPs was on a massive scale compared with anything which had previously been experienced in the

UK, and the prefix Wittekind became a household word, particularly in the south of England where most of her puppies found homes.

Mineke Mills de Hoog was the first person to import solid liver GSPs into the UK, and she subsequently concentrated her breeding in that direction. Irus von der Saarner Mark, later to become Aust. Ft. and Rt. Ch., came through her hands en route for Australia. He made no impression here in show or field but was used prolifically at stud to Wittekind bitches, and produced many Champions. Wittekind breeding produced the following Champions:

Sh. Ch. Wittekind Felicity (Irus v d Saarner Mark – Appeline Juniper)
Ch. Wittekind Gregory (Irus v d Saarner Mark – Connie von der Arrierveldon – Imp.)
Sh. Ch. Wittekind Hannibal (Ch. Wittekind Gregory – Appeline Juniper)
Ch. Wittekind Erica (Irus v d Saarner Mark – Kleiner Helga – Imp.)
Sh. Ch. Wittekind Happy Harpo (Ch. Wittekind Gregory – Connie v d Arrierveldon)
Sh. Ch. Wittekind Fredrick (Irus v d Saarner Mark – Appeline Juniper)
Sh. Ch. Wittekind Edelstein (Irus v d Saarner Mark – Kleiner Helga)
Ch. Wittekind Igor (Irus v d Saarner Mark – Connie v d Arriervelden)
Sh. Ch. Wittekind Solveig (Joep – Imp. – Ch. Wittekind Erica)
Sh. Ch. Pandora of Wittekind (Ch. Wittekind Igor – Kleiner Helga)
Sh. Ch. Pepita of Wittekind (Ch. Wittekind Igor – Kleiner Helga)
Ft. Ch. Skyhigh Jonny of Wittekind (Ch. Wittekind Gregory – Wittekind Katika)
Sh. Ch. Wittekind Nelson (Wittekind Ivanhof – Wittekind Elenor)
Sh. Ch. Wittekind Inca Zoltowski (Huntsman Hector – Sh. Ch. Pandora of Wittekind)
Ch. Wittekind Donner (Ft. Ch. Skyhigh Jonny of Wittekind – Wittekind Chocolate Candy)
Sh. Ch. Wittekind Russ (Ch. Wittekind Donner – Wittekind Sleeping Beauty).

Wittekind was the prefix of either the sire or the dam of:
Sh. Ch. Carrigtemple Little Auk (D) Appeline Wittekind Francine.
Ch. Adrem Nicholas (S) Wittekind Edward.
Ch. and Ft. Ch. Mathams Dark Claret of Trolanda (S) Ch. Wittekind Gregory.
Sh. Ch. and Can. Ch. Quarryhall Furry William (S) Ch. Wittekind Igor.
Sh. Ch. Trakevlyn Braun Baron (S) Ch. Wittekind Hannibal. (D) Hedda Wittekind.
Sh. Ch. Isara Kurzhaar Antler (S) Wittekind Franz (D) Sh. Ch. Patricks Piper of Wittekind.
Sh. Ch. Isara Kurzhaar Archer (S) Wittekind Franz (D) Sh. Ch. Patricks Piper of Wittekind.
Ch. Isara Kurzhaar Alpe (S) Wittekind Franz (D) Sh. Ch. Patricks Piper of Wittekind.
Sh. Ch. Bellandowa Cirio (S) Wittekind Zeppelin.
Ft. Ch. Trakevlyn Commanchero (S) Ch. Wittekind Hannibal (D) Hedda Wittekind.
Sh. Ch. Newsirs Paddock (S) Sh. Ch. Wittekind Happy Harpo.
Sh. Ch. Hillanhi Hjordis (D) Sh. Ch. Wittekind Solveig.
Sh. Ch. Christingham Arden Blaze (S) Gregorius of Wittekind.
Sh. Ch. Isara Kurzhaar Hoopoe (D) Sh. Ch. Patricks Piper of Wittekind.
Sh. Ch. Stoneways Zanlander (S) Sh. Ch. Pepita of Wittekind.
Sh. Ch. Christingham Azalea Mist (S) Gregorius of Wittekind.
Sh. Ch. Booton Olaf (D) Wittekind Rosa Linda.
Sh. Ch. Waldburg Dino (S) Ch. Wittekind Gregory.
Sh. Ch. Subar Appollo of Warringah (S) Sh. Ch. Wittekind Inca Zoltowski.
Sh. Ch. Isara Kurzhaar Keeper of Grakimor (S) Ft. Ch. Skyhigh Jonny of Wittekind. (D) Sh. Ch. Patricks Piper of Wittekind.

Sh. Ch. Field Maple (S) Sh. Ch. Wittekind Inca Zoltowski.
Sh. Ch. Isara Kurzhaar Champignone (D) Sh. Ch. Patricks Piper of Wittekind.
Sh. Ch. Bellandowa Ballerina (S) Ft. Ch. Skyhigh Jonny of Wittekind.
Sh. Ch. Gavalie Czofia (S) Ch. Wittekind Gregory (D) Wittekind Ursula.
Sh. Ch. Isara Kurzhaar Hilde (D) Sh. Ch. Patricks Piper of Wittekind.

HILLANHI
Jean Bates started with a Wittekind bitch, Sh. Ch. Wittekind Solveig, and a Midlander dog, Ch. Midlander Peer Gynt. Her breeding programme has produced the top CC winning GSP, Sh. Ch. Hillanhi Hjordis with over forty CCs, and several other Champions:
Sh. Ch. Hillanhi Hjordis (Ch. Midlander Peer Gynt – Sh. Ch. Wittekind Solveig)
Sh. Ch. Hillanhi Tanne (Sh. Ch. Galahad of Booton – Sh. Ch. Hillanhi Hjordis)
Sh. Ch. Hillanhi Laith (Sh. Ch. Inchmarlo Montana – Sh. Ch. Hillanhi Hjordis)
Sh. Ch. Hillanhi Helvern of Badgebree (Sh. Ch. Hillanhi Tanne – Sh. Ch. Hillanhi Laith)
Sh. Ch. Hillanhi Hejne of Helydon (Sh. Ch. Miroku Anton from Dallyvista – Sh. Ch. Hillanhi Laith)

ISARA KURZHAAR.
Early in the 1970s another lady of European birth, Mrs Fio Roberts began her prodigious breeding programme, based on Wittekind stock. Looking at the registrations which followed, you might be forgiven for thinking that this lady had a compulsion to overtake the record established by Wittekind. In any event, the result has been a huge number of Champions of one standing or another, carrying this prefix. They are:
Sh. Ch. Isara Kurzhaar Archer (Wittekind Franz – Sh. Ch. Patricks Piper of Wittekind)
Ch. Isara Kurzhaar Alpe (Wittekind Franz –Sh. Ch. Patricks Piper of Wittekind)

*Denise Gatliffe's
Ch. Geramer's
Suhaili.*

Sh. Ch. Isara Kurzhaar Antler (Wittekind Franz – Sh. Ch. Patricks Piper of Wittekind)

Sh. Ch. Isara Kurzhaar Hexe (Starlites Greif von Kasia – Imp. – Sh. Ch. Patricks Piper of Wittekind)

Sh. Ch. Isara Kurzhaar Hoopoe and Sh. Ch. Isara Kurzhaar Hilde, both by Starlites Greif von Kasia out of Sh. Ch. Patricks Piper of Wittekind.

Sh. Ch. Isara Kurzhaar Ceili (Isara Kurzhaar Harrier – Quarryhall Moonrays of Isara)

Sh. Ch. Isara Kurzhaar Viper, Sh. Ch. Isara Kurzhaar Vielle and Sh. Ch. Isara Kurzhaar Victualler, all by Sh. Ch. Am Ch. and Aust. Ch. Adams Hagen von Waldenburg out of Sh. Ch. Isara Kurzhaar Ceili.

Ch. Isara Kurzhaar Xanthippe (Isara Kurzhaar Merganser – Sh. Ch. Isara Kurzhaar Hoopoe)

Sh. Ch. Isara Kurzhaar Drambuie, Sh. Ch. Isara Kurzhaar Ricewine, and Sh. Ch. Isara Kurzhaar Liquer, all by Sh. Ch. Isara Kurzhaar Victualler out of Sh. Ch. Isara Kurzhaar Hoopoe.

Sh. Ch. Isara Kurzhaar Champignone (Sh. Ch. Isara Kurzhaar Victualler – Sh. Ch. Patricks Piper of Wittekind.)

Sh. Ch. Isara Kurzhaar Xflame, Sh. Ch. Isara Kurzhaar Vintage, and Ir. Ch. Isara Kurzhaar Vintener, all by Sh. Ch. Isara Kurzhaar Victualler out of Isara Kurzhaar Queenie.

Sh. Ch. Isara Kurzhaar Xylophone (Isara Kurzhaar Merganser – Sh. Ch. Isara Kurzhaar Hoopoe)

Sh. Ch. Isara Kurzhaar Treacle (Sh. Ch. Field Maple –Sh. Ch. Isara Kurzhaar Champignone)

Ch. Isara Kurzhaar Hellfire at Alcazar (Isara Kurzhaar Tapdancer – Sh. Ch. Isara Kurzhaar Ricewine)

Sh. Ch. Isara Kurzhaar Merganser (Ch. and Ft. Ch. Swifthouse Tufty – Isara Kurzhaar Antje)

Sh. Ch. Isara Kurzhaar Keeper of Grakimor (Ft. Ch. Skyhigh Jonny of Wittekind – Sh. Ch. Patricks Piper of Wittekind.)

Additionally, each of the following Champions owe to Isara Kurzhaar through their sire or dam:

Ch. Geramers Victress of Swifthouse (D) Ch. Isara Kurzhaar Alpe.

Ch. Geramers Cromarty of Swifthouse (D) Ch. Isara Kurzhaar Alpe.

Ch. Geramers Sea Venom (D) Ch. Isara Kurzhaar Alpe.

Sh. Ch. Kritzman Beva (S) Sh. Ch. Isara Kurzhaar Victualler (D) Sh. Ch. Isara Kurzhaar Hexe.

Ch. Geramers Suhaili (D) Ch. Isara Kurzhaar Alpe.

Ch. and Ft. Ch. Geramers Shannon (D) Ch. Isara Kurzhaar Alpe.

Sh. Ch. Rypoint Oona (S) Sh. Ch. Isara Kurzhaar Victualler.

Sh. Ch. Barleyarch Panther (D) Ch. Isara Kurzhaar Xanthippe.

Sh. Ch. Kritzman Biggles (S) Sh. Ch. Isara Kurzhaar Victualler (D) Sh. Ch. Isara Kurzhaar Hexe.

Sh. Ch. Mistyayre Bucks Fizz (S) Sh. Ch. Isara Kurzhaar Archer.

Sh. Ch. Jennaline Kentish Crumpet (D) Isara Kurzhaar Lucozade.

Sh. Ch. Wyndcliffe Virginia (S) Isara Kurzhaar Helfer.

Sh. Ch. Easemore Mitchy Girl (D) Isara Kurzhaar Limeade.

Sh. Ch. Kritzman Abba (S) Sh. Ch. Isara Kurzhaar Archer (D) Sh. Ch. Isara Kurzhaar Hexe.

BIRKENWALD

The early 1970s saw yet another new prefix coming to the forefront – once again owned by a lady of European blood. Mrs A. Spoors, later Mrs Gill, made a name for herself and her breeding. Birkenwald was to stand with Isara Kurzhaar and Wittekind as another of the big producing kennels. Using an imported sire, namely Can. Ch. Ulda Evan von Offa, as mate to several bitches she began to produce many GSPs and some Champions. Her interest at first was apparently restricted to aiming for success in the show ring, but she soon came to recognise the importance of the working side of the breed, and she turned to trialing with some good results. Her Champions included:

Sh. Ch. Birkenwald Ilka (Can. Ch. Ulda Evan von Offa – Birkenwald Christina)
Sh. Ch. Birkenwald Gerhard (Birkenwald Anton – Birkenwald Della)
Sh. Ch. Birkenwald Kyra (Can. Ch. Ulda Evan von Offa – Birkenwald Della)
Sh. Ch. Birkenwald Mandel (Birkenwald Janus – Birkenwald Glocka).

Birkenwald blood was also responsible in part for Sh. Ch. Waldburg Dino whose dam was Sh. Ch. Birkenwald Mandel and who was bred by Miss C. Spoors, Mrs Gill's daughter. Mrs Gill later turned her interest to black and white GSPs and has imported and bred a good many, but neither she nor anyone else has produced a B/W champion in the UK to date. She was, however, instrumental in the first B/W import to Australia, where that colour has had greater popularity and success.

BARLEYARCH
Mrs S. Harris' Barleyarch prefix has been one of the more successful newer producers. Based on sound Isara Kurzhaar stock, she has produced several Show Champions, and, being aware of the desirability, is now proving that her stock can work by gaining their full title. Her breeding includes:

Sh. Ch. Barleyarch Painted Lady (Sh. Ch. Stormridge Midnight – Ch. Isara Kurzhaar Xanthippe)
Ch. Barleyarch Platinum (Sh. Ch. Isara Kurzhaar Archer – Ch. Isara Kurzhaar Xylophone)
Sh. Ch. Barleyarch Tiger and Sh. Ch. Barleyarch Panther, both by Sh. Ch. Inchmarlo Montana out of Ch. Isara Kurzhaar Xanthippe.
Sh. Ch. Barleyarch Polka (Ch. and Ft. Ch. Stairfoot Sobrig – Ch. Barleyarch Platinum).

Sh. Ch. Barleyarch Polka: Our Dogs/Pedigree Chum Top sire 1992.

OTHER LEADING KENNELS

Despite a dozen or so new imports since the 1950s, the gene pool in the UK is still small, and by far the greater proportion of 'top dogs' relate in some degree to that very small originally imported stock. This must be a factor which has affected breeding and accounts for the fact that the breed type in UK is so singular.

In reviewing the big producing kennels, you can also see that there have been many smaller but invaluable contributions made by less vigorous breeders. Mr W. Wade bred Ch. Mordax Morning Mist, Ch. Larberry Link and Sh. Ch. Larberry Fern. All these were owned by Jane, daughter of Bettie Farrand, who campaigned them. Bettie Farrand is, of course, a name of great fame in the breed of Wire-haired Dachshunds. All three owed to Weedonbrook and Nevern. Among others in the early years were Geoffrey Sterne, long-time President of the GSP Club, and John Gassman, owner of Ch. Zita Sand and Ch. Blitz of Longsutton, the latter bred by Mr Sterne. Brian Mettam bred the Littlestats, and the Cellerhof and Springfarm offspring of the Johnsons and the Middletons all fitted into the early breeding programme.

Mrs Louise Petrie-Hay started her Waidman strain with Ch. Littlestat Condiment. She was later instrumental in the popularization of black and white GSPs, and many Waidmans are of that colour. Friuli GSPs started in ownership of Mr Zanussi and passed to his son-in-law, Mr F. Musslewhite, and the records show that he has had considerable success in Field Trials but not in the show-ring. Douglas and Carol Appleton, world-famous in hounds, bred a few good GSPs, particularly Sh. Ch. Appeline Chough who was an influential sire of his day.

Trolanda, the prefix owned by Mr A.Ashton, Mathams owned by Mr J. Kew, and Monttaber owned by Brian and Jean Botterman have intermingled with some success: this is in a relatively small way in breeding terms but in a big way in Field Trials and show competition. The partnership which produced the two 'duals', Cliff and Madge Simons, have been at the fore in producing dual-purpose dogs, primarily from Inchmarlo and Isara Kurzhaar stock. Their prefix, Swifthouse, is now a household name amongst GSP field trialers in particular. Their dedication has produced several Ft. Champions.

Alongside these prefixes can be added a few others including Quintana, the successful dual-purpose producing kennel of that great enthusiast and hard-working Association F.T. Secretary, Maureen Nixon. There are also a number of ardent breed supporters, personified perhaps by Geoff and Deirdre Thompson and their Marklander prefix. They are not leading breeders, producing a litter only when they want another puppy for themselves, but they have bred conscientiously to maintain the best inherited characteristics of our breed. They, and others like them, play a big part in the organisation and day-to-day running of the breed societies: they are the backbone of our sport and play just as important a part in the the welfare of our breed as do the leading breeders.

Booton and Christingham are two others which have been successful prefixes, and naturally new breeders emerge every year in this increasingly popular breed. In alphabetical order, the following spring to mind: Allezwick, Ardenside, Bellandowa, Bryburn, Dorntanza (this prefix owned by the up-and-coming Trevor and Barbara Rigby, who promise to become a leading force in the breed), Gunroyd, Jennaline, Jetsanna, Levendel, Pitlea, Prusso and Questor.

All of these, and more, can be increasingly seen at competitive events. Good luck to their owners! Most of them are treading what by now is a well-worn path and they owe a great deal to the early pioneer breeders who produced the sound stock from which they can hopefully breed even better GSPs. It is my fervent hope that the newcomers will accept that old German adage, 'through performance to type'. That has proved to be the correct maxim for breeders of German Shorthaired Pointers in the past, and will stand them in good stead in the future.

Denise Gatliffe's Ch. and Ft.Ch. Geramer's

Phil and Wendy Pepper's Ch. and Ft.Ch. Stairfoot Sobrig.

Cliff and Madge Simons' Ch. and Ft.Ch. Swifthouse Tufty.

Alan Brookes' Ch. and Ft.Ch. Keldy White Knight.

Brian and Jean Botterman's Ch. and Ft. Ch. Axter's Tochter.

C.Cook.

THE DUAL CHAMPIONS

The breed scene in the UK cannot be reviewed without giving special mention to those few GSPs to attain the dual title of Champion and Field Trial Champion. This double title is obviously very difficult to achieve: the system here dictates that. The very fact that German Shorthaired Pointers have been the only breed attaining the dual title in the past forty-odd years, from all the gundog breeds here, speaks for itself.

The successful dogs deserve credit. They are:

Mrs Nora Sladden's Ch. and Ft. Ch. Inchmarlo Graff Greiff of Praha (Fritz of Praha – Deanslane Daystar of Praha)

Mrs Jean Botterman's Ch. and Ft. Ch. Axter's Tochter (Jangrath Wee Darius – Liz of Pillethcourt)

Mr Tony Ashton's Ch. and Ft. Ch. Mathams Dark Claret of Trolanda (Ch. Wittekind Gregory – Inchmarlo Dark Damsel)

Mrs Madge Simons' Ch. and Ft. Ch. Swifthouse Tufty (Fyneside Bromus – Inchmarlo Donenji)

Mr and Mrs John Gatliffe's Ch. and Ft. Ch. Geramers Shannon (Ch. and Ft. Ch. Swifthouse Tufty – Ch. Isara Kurzhaar Alpe)

Mr and Mrs Cliff Simons' Ch. and Ft. Ch. Geramers Victress of Swifthouse (Ch. and Ft. Ch. Swifthouse Tufty – Ch. Isara Kurzhaar Alpe)

Mr Alan Brookes' Ch. and Ft. Ch. Keldy White Knight (Mathams Choire –Trolanda Gull-billed Tern)

Mr and Mrs Phil Pepper's Ch. and Ft. Ch. Stairfoot Sobrig (Ch. Inchmarlo Fodhla – Hillanhi Vyatka).

It is worth noting that two of these dogs, namely Tufty and Victress, were both trained and handled by Madge and Cliff Simons – a great achievement. Many of the early breeders and owners are no longer with us, and others of us are getting older! It will be interesting to see how the breed develops in the next decade or so, and which of the newer prefixes will become GSP household names in the 21st Century.

Chapter Thirteen

THE REST OF THE WORLD

It is almost certain that we would find a scattering of German Shorthaired Pointers in the most unlikely corners of the world. Indeed, there are more countries, states and districts which have their own breed club than might be imagined. The breed is biddable, has an equable temperament, a clean, short coat and attractive outline. But above all, GSPs offer a practicality and versatility in hunting which is second to none in the gundog world. These are the real reasons why the breed is popular.

EUROPE
The German Shorthaired Pointer, unquestionably the national gundog of Germany, is held in high esteem throughout that land. The breed club effects rigorous controls over breeding; and the trial requirements, while individually suited to the activities of German hunters, demand physical quality in the winners in a way which is not found anywhere else in the world. But inevitably, the breed has not remained the prerogative of the game-shooting enthusiasts of Germany alone.

The GSP has spilled over all the national borders of Europe. The fact that Germany, positioned almost centrally in Europe, was the 'birthplace' of the GSP, made it easy for the breed to spread and to become popular in every country from Greece to the UK. Also, because there are no restrictive quarantine laws between many countries in Europe other than the UK, there is every reason for GSPs to have become a part of the general gundog scene right across the continent.

GSPs are very strongly represented in the Netherlands, almost equalling Germany, and are favoured in Scandinavia. They are even popular in those countries which already have their own national utility gundog breeds. They can frequently be encountered in France, despite the fact that France has several national utility gundogs, a number of braques and the Brittany Spaniel. I have met a few in Portugal, and GSPs are certainly used to hunt partridges in Spain. The breed is popular to a degree in Italy: indeed a surprising number of people of Italian origin are owners in the USA and the UK. In fact, I suspect the GSP easily out-numbers the Italian Spinone, the Italian national utility gundog. The Midlander kennel and others have exported British stock to Greece and there are numerous GSPs owned by the sporting fraternity there.

SWEDEN, NORWAY AND FINLAND
The Swedish Vorsteh Club (SVC), a member club of the Swedish Kennel Club, was founded in 1917. It is the group breed club for all the European pointing breeds. Its purpose is to encourage the breeding of high-quality hunting dogs: mentally and physically fitting to be good all-round gundogs. The GSP and GWP are the two major breeds in SVC and are the most successful in Field

Harry Nilsson's Sh.Ch. Orrtuns Donner, Imp. Norway.

Trial competition. The Swedish registration figures (all puppies born and registered and imported dogs registered) during the past seven years are shown below. The other HPR breeds are included as a comparison, which indicates the popularity of the German Pointers. It can be seen that the Small Munsterlander and the German Longhaired Pointer both have a reasonable rating, though these breeds are not present at all in the UK. It is also interesting to note that while the annual registration of GWPs has remained relatively stable, that for GSPs has more than doubled from 1986 to 1992. It is a matter for conjecture whether the average Swedish hunter has turned (despite the advantage of the Wirehair coat in hard climatic conditions) to the Shorthair, finding it to be the ideal all-round gundog.

Breed/Year	1986	1987	1988	1989	1990	1991	1992
German Shorthaired Pointer	204	391	309	346	457	315	514
German Wirehaired Pointer	359	200	280	348	268	328	324
Small Munsterlander	294	212	186	203	283	295	289
German Longhaired Pointer	23	32	25	26	17	47	40
Hungarian Vizsla	17	11	12	18	10	19	34
Weimaraner	6	8	17	7	16	10	26
Large Munsterlander	4	11	13	8	33	38	14
Italian Spinone	10	10	0	13	1	7	10
Brittany	41	8	37	23	8	53	7

FIELD TRIALS

Geographically, Sweden is a 'long' country, some 1600 km (994 miles) from north to south. The difference between the south and the north is great when considering climate, terrain and hunting traditions. The Swedish GSP must, therefore, be capable of working in very different hunting situations.

*Randi
Johansson's Dual
Ch. Geggens
Nadja, Imp.
Norway.*

The purpose of Field Trials is to test the dog's ability to hunt, point and retrieve. Great emphasis is put on the fact that trials should be like a real hunting day. For example, any partridge or pheasants reared and released must be 'wild' for at least two weeks before being hunted.

There are three classes of trial:

Junior: for dogs under 24 months of age.

Open: for dogs not having won more than one first prize in open class.

Elite: for dogs having more than one first prize in open classes.

The trials are split into four parts and a dog must be approved in all four sections to get a prize. The sections are:

FIELD AND RETRIEVE: Because of the variation of terrain in the country, this test can take place in any one of three different circumstances.

a. High mountain (alp) where white grouse (Lagopus Lagopus) is the game.

b. Forest (spruce and pine) where black grouse and capercaillie (wood grouse) are the game.

c. 'Field' where pheasant and partridge are the game.

This has a parallel in the UK where we hold trials on high moorland and the game is red grouse or black game; or on English lowland where the game is pheasant and/or partridge.

The dog is required to hunt to find game, to point staunchly, to produce the game, to be steady to shot and fall, and to retrieve on command any shot game. Junior dogs are allowed a degree of disobedience, providing they work hard to get game by scent. Alternatively, Elite dogs must show complete obedience and be outstanding as gundogs in every respect. To get 8 points or more, the dog must work for about 60 minutes and at least one bird must be shot and retrieved. If no birds are shot on during the dog's run, a retrieve of a thrown bird is arranged. It is not unusual that the gun is carried by the judge, as might be on a shooting day.

WATER TEST: For Juniors the dog has to sit free at the handler's side while a dead bird (usually a

Sven Runberg's Ch. Randolph retrieving a white grouse.

seagull) is thrown from the shore into open water. The retrieve must only be made on command. For Open dogs the bird is thrown and a shot is fired from a boat. The bird must fall into reeds at 40-60 metres from the shore. After demonstrating steadiness, the dog must retrieve the bird on command. For Elite dogs the retrieve is similar to the open but the retrieve is 'blind'. The handler is informed of the position of the bird in the reeds and the dog retrieves on command and direction of the handler.

TRACKING TEST: For Juniors a bird (a dead seagull or grouse) or a rabbit is dragged 150 metres into the forest. The dog has to follow the track and retrieve the game to the starting place. The handler is allowed to follow the dog. For Open dogs the track is similar, but 200 metres long, and the handler is not allowed to follow, so the dog has to work alone to bring the game back to the handler at the starting point. For Elite dogs the test is exactly as for the Open, but the game used is a beast of prey, for example a fox.

In each section a dog may get a maximum 10 points. These have a coefficient applied as follows:

	Coeff.	Max points	
Field	10	100	First Prize 160 to 200 points.
Water	5	50	Second Prize 120 to 159 points
Track	3	30	Third Prize 80 to 119 points.
Retrieve	2	20	

It can be seen that the major emphasis is put upon field and water work.

BLOOD TRACKING TEST: This is the same for all breeds. The dog has to follow a blood track which is 600 metres long and is three hours old. Dogs which pass the test are deemed to be qualified trackhounds for wounded big game (i.e. elk and deer). Such dogs must be available for big game hunting, according to Swedish law.

THE SHOW SCENE
Dogs can be exhibited at shows licensed by the Swedish Kennel Club, at All breed shows or at Specialty breed shows organised by SVC. The showing of GSPs in Sweden is not very popular. In order to get a Challenge Certificate the dog must have a Field Trial qualification.

The Champion titles available to GSPs in Sweden are as follows:

Randi Olofsson's Dual Ch. Erssjons A-Centha.

Inge Hansen's Int. Ch. Duke.

SHOW CHAMPION (Sh.Ch.): Three CCs at shows, at least one being after the dog is two years of age. Additionally, the dog must have a first prize in an open Field Trial.

INTERNATIONAL SHOW CHAMPION (Int. Ch.): Two CACIBs, at least one year between the two awards. Additionally, the dog must have a first prize in an open Field Trial.

FIELD TRIAL CHAMPION (FT CH.): Two first prizes in Elite class Field Trials, a pass in Bloodtrack, and at least a second prize in an open class at a show (proving the dog to be of good type).

Thus no Swedish dog can become a Champion without gaining both Field Trial and show awards. The following list illustrates the comparatively small number of dogs to attain title (because of these strict requirements) since 1980. They are all Swedish-owned, but the N before the year of birth indicates that they were born in Norway.

*Carin Ahlstedt's
Dual Ch. Dierges
Bertil.*

DUAL CHAMPION (FT. Ch. and Sh. Ch.)
The finest title a Swedish GSP can obtain:
Aska, 1984) (Int. Ch. Duke – Dual Ch. Granhagens Brontemacdess).
Caesar, 1981 (Ch. Tello – Collette).
Charlie, 1983 (Firhouse Aelfgar – Norrskenets Cheri).
Caby's Daisy, 1981 (Ft. Ch. Kongstorps Aro – Caby's Aniara).
Dierges Bertil, N 1984 (Erf Vom Osterberg – Moyfrid).
Errsjons A-Centha, 1987 (Int. Ch. Osbakkens Tex – Carra).
Ex, 1985 (Dual Ch. Charlie – Tosterons Goldy).
Fay, 1982 (Ch. Fiolmyrans Dog – Caby's Betty-Boop).
Fredmakens Hast,1983 (Ft. Ch. Nero – Ch. Fredmarkens Trixa).
Fredmarkens Raska, 1985 (Ft. Ch. Nero – Ch. Fredmarkens Trixa).
Fredmarkens Raxa, 1983 (Ft. Ch. Nero – Ch. Fredmarkens Trixa).
Gangster, 1984 (Unos Rothenuffeln – Tosterons Snabba).
Geggens Nadja, N1986 (Erf Vom Osterberg – Geggens Farrah).
Gry, 1984 (Lundars Aslak – Lia).
Kubens Elite, 1985 (Ch. Klover Knekt Tilbrekt – Ch. Sussi).
Norrskenets Fozberry, 1980 (Dual Ch. Ravatj Ego – Ripmarkens Jakta).
Querida, N1987 (Ch. Rugdelias BCT Tonca – Maxa).
Sniff, 1987 (Ft. Ch. Hugo – Cobra).

FIELD TRIAL CHAMPIONS (FT. CH.).
Boy, 1986 (Dual Ch. Caesar – Dual Ch. Granhagens Brontemacdess).
Gustav, 1985 (Ch. Eiterdalens Bra – Twiggy).
Hugo, N 1984 (Unos Rothenuffeln – Tosterons Skutta).

Birger Lnutsson's Dual Ch. Sniff.

INTERNATIONAL AND SHOW CHAMPIONS (INT. CH. AND SH. CH.).
Bondbonans Spexa 1984 (Dual Ch. Pedro – Tosterons Snoa).
Cliff, 1981 (Ch. Tello – Collette).
Caby's Jeffie, 1987 (Ch. Klover Knekt Tilbrekt – Int. Ch. Nimba).
Granhagens Lillefixbydess, 1981 (Int. Ch. Ajax –Inchmarlo Dess).
Krutgubbens Barry,1980 (Killer – Bessy).
Nimba, 1982 (Caby's Churchill – Lorry).
Osbakkens Tex, N 1985 (Calle – Osbakkens Raya).
Rypeheias Tikki, N 1981 (Dual Ch. Ravatj Ego – Ripmarkens K-Tikki).
Tiia, 1985 (Int. Ch. Caby's Belsebub – Jill).
Vargvilans Fusca, 1984 (Int. Ch. Duke – Chiawata's Agda).
Vantans Gilla, 1985 (Int. Ch. Duke – Fredmarkens Prillan).

*Ann-Sophie
Rundberg's Int.
Ch. Nimba.*

SHOW CHAMPIONS (SH. CH.)
Anja, 1988 (Dual Ch. Kvarsteinens Nicky – Bessi).
Arrak 1989 (Dual Ch. Fay – Jagdmeisters Cista).
Asumdalens Ticki, 1986 (Ch. Kubens Degaulle – Penny).
Athos-X, 1985 (Firhouse Aelfgar – E-Tassa av Vestgarden).
Brickegardens Balder, 1983 (Tosterons Fritz – Dollan).
Brickegardens Caruso, 1986 (Ripmarkens Lex – Brickegardens Lotta).
Callit, 1987 (Ch. Klover Knekt Tilbrekt – Int. Ch. Tiia).
Carmen, 1987 (Ch. Klover Knekt Tilbrekt – Int. Ch. Tiia).
Cintha, 1984 (Ch. Lassie – Kubens Viva).
Caby's Hebbe, 1985 (Dual Ch. Caesar – Dual Ch. Caby's Daisy).
Caby's Obelix, 1990 (Caby's Jacko – Dual Ch. Caby's Daisy).
Donna, 1987 (Sarek –Jarpkullens Citty).
E'Cora, 1985 (Dual Ch. Charlie – Tosterons Goldy).
Eddy, 1983 (Ft. Ch. Nero – Ch. Lola).
Eiterdalens Bra, N 1981 (Snob – Jenki).
Fotevikens Gina, 1985 (Ft. Ch. Hugo – Tellus Tella).
Fredmarkens Basta, 1983 (Ft. Ch. Nero – Ch. Fredmarkens Trixa).
Fredmarkens Haxa, 1983 (Ft. Ch. Nero – Ch. Fredmarkens Trixa).
Fredmarkens Ilo, 1983 (Ft. Ch. Nero – Ch. Fredmarkens Trixa).
Granhagens Asterixbydess, 1981 (Int. Ch. Ajax – Inchmarlo Dess).
Humla, 1987 (Dual Ch. Charlie – Tosterons Snabba).
Jamba, 1980 (Ripmarkens Jazz – Raja).
Jarkpullens Ax, 1982 (Dual Ch. Snelias Ali – Ch. Tosterons Rumba).
Knoppetorpets Heisy, 1985 (Ft. Ch. Hugo – Jonskollens Easy).

Ann-Sophie Rundberg's Ch. Caby's Obelix.

Linkopia.

Kompis, 1985 (Ch. Cliff – Ilona).
Krutgubbens Deja, 1982 (Killer – Bessy).
Kubens Degaulle, 1983 (Dual Ch. Pedro – Ch. Sussi).
Mirro, 1981 (Ch. Lassie – Mikra).
Mixa, 1981 (Ch. Lassie – Mikra).
Mon-Ami av Dahlwinn, N 1986 (Ch. Brickegardens Balder – Lundars Twiggy).
Masans Disney, N 1988 (Rauhreif vom Kege-Haus – Geggens Jenny).
Nimbus, 1982 (Caby's Churchill – Lorry).
Nunnesikens Mattis, 1987 (Int. Ch. Fredmarkens Hast – Ch. Mixa).
Nunneskins Traj, 1984 (Moltas – Ch. Mixa).
Orrtun's Donna, N 1985 (Erf vom Osterberg – Geggens Gulla).
Pan, N 1987 (Ch. Rugdelias BCT Tonca – Maxa).
Pastastigens Ak Argos, 1989 (Rypeheias Kompis – Int. Dual Ch. Azka).
Perdica Fixa, 1988 (Ch. Rugdelias BCT Tonca – Dual Ch. Fredmarkens Raxa).
Perla, N 1983 (Ch. Bask – Fanta).
Raisa, 1990 (Ch. Falko von der Reiterstadt – Caby's Hilda).
Randolf, 1990 (Ch. Falko von der Reiterstadt – Caby's Hilda).
Revhedens ecco, 1988 (Ch. Orrtun's Donner – Knoppetorpets Zetti).
Ronja, 1987 (Int. Ch. Caby's Belsebub – Maja).
Ravatj Major, 1982 (Dual Ch. Snelias Ali –Dual Ch. Ravatj Faba).
Ravatj Minus, 1982 (Dual Ch. Snelias Ali – Dual Ch. Ravatj Faba).
Ravatj Recta, 1984 (Dual Ch. Snelias Ali – Dual Ch. Ravatj Faba).
Sakka, 1983 (Ch. Norrskenets Chipps – Tosterons Polka).
Skimmelns Aida, 1988 (Ch. Athos-X – Ch. Mon-Ami av Dahlwinn).
Skimmelns Carmen, 1989 (Ch. Athos-X – Muffi).

Eleven holders of Field Trial awards – six of them are Champions.

Skimmelns Curry, 1989 (Ch. Athos-X – Muffi).
Snelias Ceb, N 1982 (Dual Ch. Ravatj Ego – Gaya).
Tarri, 1984 (Ch. Lassie – Kubens Viva).
Tellus Ullman, 1980 (Tellus Rebell – Tellus Stella).
Tosterons Jazza, 1986 (Firhouse Aelfgar – Tosterons Goldy).
Tosterons Snabba, 1980 (Dual Ch. Zacko – Dual Ch. Ripmarkens Mecca).
Tray, 1986 (Broman – Bonnie).
Trixa, 1988 (Zacko – A-ca-pella).
Tradgransens Cederlund, 1983 (Traskviddens Bas – Stina).
Uggelboets Dixi, 1988 (Ch. Eddy – Ch. Cintha).
Videviddens Unos, 1989 (Ft. Ch. Cimbrohs Uncas – Int. Ch. Rypeheias Tikka).
Vittringens Jerry, 198 (Caby's Amigo – Hera).
Vittringens Jina, 1982 (Caby's Amigo – Hera).
Vantans Gnuttan, 1985 (Int. Ch. Duke – Fredmarkens Prillan).
Zita, 1986 (Ajax – Netta).

BREEDING IN SWEDEN.
Most GSP breeders of this country are not big producers, having a few litters from their starter-bitch and continuing by keeping a daughter to breed from in due course, and so on. Regrettably, as everywhere in the world, there are some breeders who do not have regard for the working aspect of the breed and do not enter field trials. Many do not even use their GSPs for practical gundog work.

Sweden, Norway and Finland have been isolated since the late 1960s due to to rabies. In 1988 Finland was closed to Sweden and Norway because they had one case of rabies. Quarantine is expensive (about £2,000 sterling) but there has been some importation of male dogs.

Seven German dogs have been imported to Norway. They have been used at stud in both Norway and Sweden. To date, only Falko von dem Reiterstadt has attained Championship status. The list is as follows:

Olav vom Pregelufer N03054/81 (by Elk v Hegehaus – Festa v Pregelufer).
Unos Rothenuffeln N05651/81 (Ingen von Sixenhof – Jutta v Gruntal).
Erf vom Osterberg N05650/81 (Tell v Osterberg – Dunja vd Eidermuhle).
Rauhreif vom Hege-haus N12400/87 (Helfer v Hege-haus – Walda v Niestetal).
Sh. Ch. Falko vd Reiterstadt N34903/86 (Remo Rothenuffeln – Cora vd Reiterstadt).
Dax vom Weisenbach N30173/90 (Ziro vom Mariahoeh – Yanka vom Mariahoeh).
Moritz vom Westermoor N27525/91 (Emir Rothenuffeln – Freia vom Pulverberg).

SWEDISH IMPORTS
Firhouse Aelfgar N11337/82 – from England (Eng.Sh.Ch. Am.Ch. Aust. Ch. Adams Hagen von Waldenburg – Eng. Ch. Firhouse Mountain Ringlet). This dog was imported and owned by Tommy Andersson, of Jokkmokk. Aelfgar is known as Kallega and has won several prizes in Field Trials. The list of Champion shows that he is the sire of three Champions, and he is also grandsire of eight Champions.

Aust. Ch. Kazia Chances Are S55985/88 – from Australia (Birdrise Chance – Aust. Ch. Kazia Holly Holigatly). Imported by Bjorn Larsson, of Kennel Fredmarken, Chance has not been used so much. He has not been started in field trials and has no offspring with field trial awards.

Burnbrook Garganey S49079/91 – from Australia (Burnbrook Umfolozi – Burnbrook the Panther).

In Autumn 1992 'Gally' received second prize in an Open Field Trial. The trial was in the high mountain (alps) – a considerable contrast with his place of birth near Perth, West Australia! From these ten imports between 1980 and 1992 a total of 327 offspring have been registered, of which 39 have obtained Field Trial awards. As I do not have details of a similar nature for home-bred stock, comparison is not possible. In any event, it may be that only the keenest breeder/field trialers are involved with imports, and if so, their enthusiasm may affect the issue. Certainly, most of the imports have made a real contribution to the breed, which justifies the great expense of purchasing stock from abroad.

There are no great problems with breed defects here. Though entropion, epilepsy and hip dysplasia do exist in GSPs, as in all countries, careful screening and judicious breeding keeps the problems to a minimum. Only dogs with good hips are bred from, which is a good example of the careful regard for breeding only good type GSPs which is considered so important in Sweden.

NEW ZEALAND
Michael Brander exported the first GSPs to New Zealand in 1957, and since then they have expanded in the hands of an increasingly large number of breeders. There is a real interest in the use of the breed as a hunting dog, and there is a good variety of game, including pheasants, partridges, quail and rabbits, and a lot of wildfowl are shot.

On a personal note, my wife Mic and I have judged the breed at shows here several times, and we have also judged HPR trials and been involved with 'gundog and field days', shooting over the dogs. Mostly the trials are held in conjunction with Pointers and Setters. A set course is run with

Wendy Schwalger's Ch. Karlsruhe Jaime QC, CDX.

Kathy Hughes' Ch. Kazia von Jagenspeil.

caged pigeons to hunt and point and dead pigeons to find and retrieve – and stringent rules of performance. There is also a good move towards holding live game trials for HPR breeds, and it is to be hoped that this will come to fruition, so introducing a more realistic basis on which to judge the true game-finding capabilities of the dogs.

There are only a small number of active field trialers in New Zealand at present, but the introduction of wild game hunting to trials would no doubt attract some hunters who have previously declined to be associated with trials on caged pigeons. Field trialing on pheasants would present some difficulty. They are present in the wild, mostly in forest land, but although it is relatively easy to get permission to shoot, and hunting by GSP owners is popular, I believe it is illegal to shoot hen birds under any circumstances. The penalty for doing so is very severe!

Barry and Christine Hill's Ch. and Ft. Ch. Sheik of Holmbrook.

A lot of serious breeding has been done by responsible people and, among a fairly large population of dogs, there are some very good ones. GSPs are not show-exhibited in very large numbers, but the quality is consistent. There are clubs in both North and South Island. Mic has the honour to be Patron of the Continental Gundog Club, which centres on Wellington, and caters, as one might guess by the title, for all HPR breeds. There is also the Otago and Southland GSP Club, the Canterbury and Districts GSP Club, and the Auckland and Districts GSP Club; all with fair numbers of enthusiastic members, many of whom are work as well as show orientated.

In North Island, Jack Cooke's Dawnflight kennel has been a force to be reckoned with, Ch. Dawnflight Rogue being the first of only three GSPs in the Island to gain all breeds Best in Show awards. The second, now sadly dead, was Ch. Bellemay Jasper QC CDX, owned by Margaret Fowke. The third was Ch. Kazia von Jagenspeil, bred by the Butlers in Australia and owned by Kathy Hughes. He has been a great Champion and a top producer. From 1982 onwards his career brought success after success. He was best dog under Mic at the Continental Gundog Show in 1986, and Best in Show at the Aucklands and District Championship Show under Georgina Byrne.

Kathy Hughes has imported and bred many other top winning GSPs and has made a measurable contribution to the development of the breed in New Zealand. Vera Pointon (Pointon's), Mandy Punnet-Millar (Millar's Hill), Harold Francis and Gavin and Karen Wilson (Stoltzhund), and Gary and Lucinda Murch (Nightflight) are all owners of successful breeding kennels which have made their mark. However, they are only a sample of a great many more enthusiastic GSP owners and breeders who are playing a part in the establishment and continuing success of the breed.

In South Island, too, there is a strong group of enthusiasts. We met, and went hunting with owners Rose Gilbert and other keen hunters. Perhaps the major breeder now is Wendy Schwalger, a lovely lady who has bred and owned many winners, including one of the top winners in New Zealand, Ch. Karlsruhe Jaime QC CDX. This dog has had Group wins in every age group through the ranks. He also won 'in Show' awards at gundog and Specialty shows including BIS at a GSP Show. In Obedience he won classes up to Test B, attaining the title CDX and was the highest placed qualifier for the title. At GSP level he held the club Obedience cup for three years. At Field Trials Jaime was competed regularly and was awarded his qualifying certificate with a high score. He was winner at many club field days and was frequently placed in field retrieving events. His progeny are following in his footsteps.

Yet another New Zealand dog of fame is Ch. and Ft. Ch. Sheik of Holmbrook QC, owned and bred by Barry and Christine Hill. Dual Champions do not come two-a-penny in New Zealand; in fact there have been only four 'duals' in the breed history of South Island. The others have been: Ch. and Ft. Ch. Hubert of Munich QC, owned by G.Bethune; Ch. and Ft. Ch. Zigeuner 'G' Freyja QC, owned by N.Young and Ch. and Ft. Ch. Freida Vom Jagerhof, owned by J.K.Davis.

Wendy Schwalger's husband, Ken, is a very keen sportsman and hunter. He not only shoots birds, but is also a stalker for both Red Deer and the quite remarkable Thar, an imported species from the Himalayas. Living, as it does, way above the tree-line on the high snow mountain chain of the South Island, this huge animal presents the ultimate challenge to stalkers. Almost a super-human task faces the would-be stalker. He has to endure ten or maybe twenty hours of the most difficult climbing to get into the area where he can begin the stalk. If successful, to man-handle the huge carcase down to the vehicle requires exhausting effort. A mounted Thar head, hanging on the dining room wall, is a trophy to be proud of indeed. Dogs have to be pretty tough to do any of the work in New Zealand: even rabbit hunting through the rough bramble, thorn and rocky shingle of the wide, dry river beds, is hard going. It is a demanding country – an environment in which the GSP excels.

AUSTRALIA

It was something of a surprise when, as we were being introduced to the competitors before beginning to judge the 10th Anniversary Championship Show of the GSP Club of Western Australia, the announcer said that Mic and I had been involved with German Shorthaired Pointers longer than the breed had been in Australia. In fact, GSPs were not first brought in from 'next door neighbours', New Zealand. Once again it was Michael Brander who, in 1963, was the initial exporter – this time sending GSPs to Jack Thompson in Victoria. Jack has gone on to become a very major force in the promotion of the breed in both show and field.

Georgina Byrne (*Der Deutsch Kurzhaar,* 1989) states that in twenty-four years Jack's Dunfriu kennel has produced almost three hundred litters of GSPs. From those litters came a prodigious list of Champions, both Show and Field, and I imagine that there are few GSP pedigrees in Australia today that do not carry some Dunfriu blood. It could be thought that this was flooding a potential market of only about fifteen millions population, but the fact is, with or without Jack's contribution, the breed has become a very popular gundog in Australia. In her book Georgina Byrne lists over seventy relatively well-known GSP breeding kennels throughout the Australian States, giving an interesting insight into the ratio of breeders to population.

I believe there are now breed clubs in every State, but Australia is a huge country and I only have personal knowledge of GSPs in New South Wales, South Australia and Western Australia. In NSW we have seen many of the lovely GSPs bred by Lynne and Caroline Butler under their prefix Kazia, and some Klugerhund GSPs bred by the Maxwells. Those great dual-purpose breed supporters, Bill and Rita Davies, imported dogs from the UK and have bred them with success. In addition, there is a great list of prominent and successful breeders in NSW. However, due possibly to an urgent desire to breed dogs which 'stand out in the crowd' for show exhibition, there has been a noticeable trend in NSW towards the popularisation of an exaggerated type of German Shorthair, which we have regrettably seen spreading to SA and WA.

Alex and Olga Gillies' Ch. Gillbrae The Sorceress.

Michael M.Trafford.

Diana Norman's Ch. Edelhof Erasmus – the solid black Champion.

Queensland boasts a thriving GSP fraternity. The breed appeared in Queensland some seven years after its first arrival in Australia, so it has been established for many years. In that time much progress has been made, and a thriving breed club looks after the interests of GSPs and their owners. It is not easy to run a club for people living so widely spread. The State of Queensland is five times bigger than the area of Germany, and travelling a 1000 miles to a canine event is not unusual.

Diana Norman (Edelhof) owned the first black and white Champion in Australia, Ch. Burnbrook Quest, bred by Georgina Byrne in WA. When mated to the solid liver Ch. Edelhof Bittersweet, the

Alex and Reylene Smith's Ch. Heiderst Dress'd In Style.

C.S. Photography.

Garth and Anne Raymond's Ch. Birdrise Zig's Image.

C.S. Photography.

L. Phelan's Australian Triple Ch. Fallohide Loki.

Eng. Sh.Ch. Am. Ch. Aust. Ch. Adams Hagen von Waldenburg.

Four of Georgina Byrne's Champions: (left to right) Burnbrook Aphrodite; B. Kalenda; B.Quintessene; B. Circe.

litter included the first solid black GSPs in Australia. From that litter came Ch. Edelhof Erasmus, the first solid black GSP, in Australia and probably in the world, to make title. The Gillies, Olga and Alex, moved into the State from NSW in 1988. Their prefix Gillbrae has enjoyed continued success in Queensland.

Field Trials for Utility Breeds are well developed in Queensland as in other States. The first winner of the State Championships was Elio Colasimone's Ft. Ch. Bulkuru Ruby CM in 1984, who repeated the performance in in 1985 and 1987. Don Nicol made great strides in the field trial world, winning trials from 1978 onwards with Ch. Dunfiu Christy CD CM. In 1983 her daughter, Ft. Ch. Reiver Ptarmigan CM became the first GSP to gain Ft.Ch. status in Queensland.

The States of South Australia and neighbouring Victoria both have strong groups of Field Trial enthusiasts. At the instigation of Mick and Kaye Munday (Mick is now an internationally known wildlife artist), we have met many of them, and I have had the great pleasure to judge Field Trials in SA on the River Murray near Mannum, and we have both judged the breed at Championship level in South Australia. Here, Field Trials are held on set-aside, grassland and stubble paddocks, hunting for wild Stubble Quail. The dogs are put down in pairs and may or may not proceed to further rounds, according to their demonstrated capability. Almost all handlers do their own shooting, although they can ask a 'gun steward' to do this.

I enjoyed the trials immensely, although I have to say I got the impression that more emphasis was put on filling the bag than on the finesse with which that was achieved. Those who are only used to shooting high birds in the UK will perhaps be surprised to hear that you seldom, if ever, see a man shooting quail in Australia with his gun barrels even as high as parallel to the ground. Stubble Quail are exciting birds to shoot, but they rarely fly more than three or four feet above the ground.

Among the leading breeders and successful owners in SA are June and Fred Kenton with the Markheim prefix, followed by Reylene and Alex Smith, who have bred some very good GSPs under the Heiderst prefix, and latterly Anne and Garth Raymond's Vallache prefix has produced many good dogs. One of the latest recruits to the breed is Jadine Mackenzie, who has had success in both SA and WA. I am aware that there are a good many other responsible and successful breeders in SA with whom I am not acquainted.

The first GSP Club in Australia was formed in Victoria in 1965 following Jack Thompson's importations and early breeding. From humble beginnings (three litters were registered in the State in 1964), the club has gone from strength to strength, providing shows, Field Trials, training days, and a pedigree typing service. Registrations peaked in 1976 with 115 litters, but now averages about 65 litters annually. A total of 160 GSPs in the State of Victoria have gained show Championship titles and 31 have become Field Trial Champions. Ten have become Duals, and one has the distinction of being a triple (show, field and retrieving) Champion.

Western Australia is sited in massive isolation as far as inter-state activities go. The distance to travel to any other State for shows or trials is incredible. However, this is not a complete barrier to the real enthusiasts, and many GSP owners do visit 'the other side' to compete, often successfully, with their dogs. There is certainly a thriving band of members of the GSP Club of WA, of which I am honoured to be co-Patron with Jack Thompson. Owners of GSPs in this State are currently going through something a crisis as far as field work is concerned. The authorities have put a stop to both quail and duck shooting – the two main sporting birds here. Trials after the fashion of those I first judged for the club in 1986 on wild quail, cannot now be run. There is naturally some difficulty in keeping the working interest alive with 'pseudo' activities. What the eventual outcome will be cannot be foreseen.

In 1992 Mic judged the GSP Club of WA Championship Show. This was a lovely show with a very good quality entry, which showed that excellent dogs are being bred in this State. BIS went to one of the top breeders, Kath Williams with her homebred Ch. Katydid The Gipsey King. Best Bitch was won by a youngster belonging to that long-distance traveller from SA, Jadine Mackenzie, who had journeyed all the way across the Nullarbor to take part in the show – that is enthusiasm for you! Among the leading breeders in this State are Kath Williams with her Katydid kennel, having countless show ring successes as well as field, her husband being a keen hunting man. Georgina Byrne, now world-famous as an author and expert in our breed, and her trial enthusiast husband, Michael, have made a huge contribution to the breed with their Burnbrook prefix.

Georgina imported Am. Ch. Eng. Sh. Ch. Aust. Ch. Adams Hagen von Waldenburg from the USA via the UK, and also Vassal vom Niestetal, the first black and white dog to come into Australia. Georgina's efforts have been instrumental in promoting the black and white (and now solid blacks) to a higher point in the popularity stakes than probably they have achieved elsewhere. Winning Burnbrooks are to be seen in nearly every record of competitive results. Robert and Wendy Bond have made their Benanee prefix famous in show and field. One of their Field Trial award winners, Ch. Benanee Keedirah, was my BIS winner in 1986. Again, a good collection of sensible breeders is scattered throughout WA. It is to be hoped that the shooting embargo can be lifted again in due course. It casts a shadow over all gundog working breeds' activities. There is really no substitute to satisfy either the hunter or his GSP.

SOUTH AFRICA
South Africa would seem to be a Mecca for working German Pointers, with huge tracts of suitable

country, and a good selection of game birds. But for some reason, the breed has not made great inroads here. We spent five weeks in South Africa in 1992, judging shows in both Western Province and Natal and also judging an all gundog breeds working gundog competitive day. Regrettably, we saw only two German Pointers, though we were assured that there are several dotted across the country, owned mainly by hunters who breed only for themselves and never think about going to a field competition or dog show.

There are no breed clubs, as far as I am aware, but several general-purpose gundog societies are happy to cater for HPR owners and have some such members who compete in retrieving competitions with Labradors and Golden Retrievers, which seem to be the most popular breeds. It would appear that there are not sufficient numbers for there to be competitions specifically for HPRs. Because the potential for the breed is so apparent, it really is surprising that it has not blossomed as it has in the Antipodes. Maybe it is just a matter of marketing, and a great number of people in South Africa are as yet unaware of the pleasures of GSP ownership which await them!

INDIA

There are several GSPs known to be in India, although not enough owners to warrant the existence of a breed club. Partridge shooting in India is not uncommon. I have a good friend, Y.P.Singh, who lives in Agra, U.P., and he tells me there is a fair enclave of GSP owners in the area. However, when dogs are not available for partridge shoots, men are used.

Y.P. writes: "We usually walk up partridges, employing men from the local village as beaters. Unfortunately, they can become very involved with the excitement of the sport, and when a bird is shot they are all likely to break ranks, running forward with shouts of joy, to make the retrieve. If a hare should be put up, they are off like a pack of hounds, and you can say goodbye to partridge shooting for that day!"

Y.P. told further how his father trained the men of one village to be completely steady, and to respond to hand and whistle signals in the field. He did not comment on their efficiency as retrievers! On some occasions, in order to increase efficiency, the beaters are tied together on a long rope at about twenty-yard intervals. They walk in a line with the rope trailing the grass, to put up the tight holding game, and the guns walk between the beaters, but just behind the trailing rope. Then, if, as his father said, the beaters run in, they can be hauled back by the guns taking hold of the rope and giving a sharp tug! What a delightful picture this conjures up!

BRAZIL

This country in South America has a GSP population, and there may well be others. One English-bred dog which made Champion in Brazil was bred by Mrs Mineke Mills de Hoog. The dog's name was Br. Ch. Wittekind Shirley's Jolian.

Chapter Fourteen

THE FUTURE

You can look at most situations from two sides, and see two differing pictures. On the one hand, it can clearly be said today that GSPs are good gundogs, that they have made their mark in the sporting world and are here to stay. Alternatively, you might consider the future of the breed, even of all gundog breeds, with some trepidation, in the light of modern attitudes to game-hunting.

That first view is the one we would all like to take. The GSP has, undoubtedly, proved its worth as an ideal dog for rough-shooters; the breed has clearly demonstrated that it is one of the most efficient game-finding utility gundogs. A specimen of this breed makes a fine family dog for those with country-loving leanings. The popularity of the breed is on the increase and promises to go from strength to strength.

Due primarily to the efforts of breed clubs, the work capability of the GSP is being kept to the forefront. Responsible breeding, by and large, keeps the breed up to standard and the physical quality of our dogs is very good: much better, frankly, than that of any of the other HPR breeds. This desirable situation holds good in every English-speaking country of the world in which I have seen GSPs. By these standards the future of the German Shorthaired Pointer can only be bright.

Most important, both for GSPs and their owners, is the simple fact that this breed has come to be appreciated for its real, rather than its imagined, virtues. The German Shorthaired Pointer is recognised in all the corners of the world as a worthwhile hunting companion. The fact that we use the dogs in slightly differing ways, according to the conditions and demands of the country we are in, matters little. It is desirable for the future of the breed that we all keep a clear view of what job of work the GSP was bred to do, and how it should be constructed to do that job most efficiently. We can all do that, recognising that we may breed and own individual dogs, but at the same time accepting that we hold the breed as a whole in trust for future hunters. That being so, and with good fortune on its side, the GSP will grace the sporting field, worldwide, in companionship with all the generations of sportsmen who are to come after we are gone.

But there is another view-point. There are world trends, not aimed directly at the GSP, but relating to, and likely to affect the breed's future. Slowly but surely, the modern world is turning 'green', and a pervasive attitude, which sides with 'protectionism' for all wildlife, is on the increase. We know that already, in at least one state of Australia, the shooting of game has been prohibited by government. The hope of a reversal of that decision is probably remote. I am reliably informed that even in Germany there have been moves to stop out of season pointing tests. Not that any birds are shot, but because other wildlife might be disturbed by handlers and dogs working across the ground!

In the UK an increasing number of people (albeit mostly unaware 'city' dwellers) are of a totally anti-blood sports persuasion, and their demonstrative activities are wrecking the legal pursuits of hunting and shooting. The situation is not improved by the the fact that an increasing number of people throughout the modern world are becoming vegetarians, and regard the killing of animals as barbaric.

Dog owners in many countries are faced with the threat of a ban on tail-docking of dogs, even for prophylactic reasons. The outcome for GSPs must be counter-productive to the use of the breed in its true role. There will only need to be a small number of dogs suffering tail damage as a result of working through close cover (which must be inevitable), before most owners will decide that the risk of injury is too great, and will cease to use their dogs in cover. The natural result will be that slowly but surely our all-purpose gundog will become 'just another pointer'.

Now bring all these threatening facts together, and the logical conclusion to be drawn is that the time can clearly be seen when all working gundogs, GSPs included, will be superfluous. The question then arises: 'Will gundogs continue to thrive by indulging in substitute activities?' The immediate answer which springs to mind is that they will not: that there is no real substitute for the reality. It it is true that many breeds, particularly in the hound group, no longer hunt their original quarry: together with their owners, Bloodhounds and Fell hounds live out, and enjoy, a false existence by hunting man-laid trails.

Perhaps the forecast of doom is not close upon us. There is hope that our traditional sports may survive and that shooting people, the true conservationists, will be left to freely enjoy their sport. We can only hope that all future gundog owners will be able to train and work dogs to even higher standards of efficiency, thus perpetuating that fabulous mystery of game-scent pointing which so endears us to the German Shorthaired Pointer.

APPENDIX

GERMAN SHORTHAIRED POINTER BREED CLUBS
Here follows a list of all the German Shorthaired Pointer Clubs I have been able to research. I am indebted to Karen Alexander, editor of the 1992-3 edition of *Bailey's Gundog Directory* (Burlington Publishing Company), and to Georgina Byrne, *Der Deutsch Kurzhaar* (Austed Publishing) for some of this information. The list shows that the breed has a very wide following throughout much of the world. Where a contact address is known, this is included.

UK
The German Shorthaired Pointer Club,
Val Grant, 30, Morrit Ave., Leeds, Yorks LS15 7EP.

The German Shorthaired Pointer Association,
Barbara Rigby, The Paddocks, Wigsley Rd., N. Scarle, Lincoln. LN6 9HD.

USA
The German Shorthaired Pointer Club of America,
Geraldine Irwin, 1101 West Quincy, Englewood, CO 80110.

Desert German Shorthaired Pointer Club,
Sue Davis, 2112 E.Aspen Dr., Tempe, AZ 85207.

Southern Arizona German Shorthaired Pointer Club,
Sue Stevenson, 8507 E.Pine Valley Dr., Tuscon, AZ 85710.

German Shorthaired Pointer Club of California,
Ada Fairchild, 4601 Briones Valley Rd., R 2, Box 174 KK. Brentwood, CA 95413

German Shorthaired Pointer Club of Central California,
Mary McDole, 333 Trapadero Dr., Salinas, CA 93906.

German Shorthaired Pointer Club of Northern Sacramento Valley,
Debbie Ferguson, 3331 Winter Park Dr., #21 Sacramento, CA 95834.

German Shorthaired Pointer Club of Orange County,
Randy Wessman, 78200 Calle Fortuna, La Quinta, CA 92253.

German Shorthaired Pointer Club of Riverside County,
Stephanie Casdorph, 28340 Live Oak Canyon Rd., Redlands, CA 92374.

German Shorthaired Pointer Club of San Diego,
Linda Abercrombie, 12744 Rancho Penasquitos Blv., San Diego, CA 92129.

German Shorthaired Pointer Club of Santa Clara Valley,
Kathy Otterlei, 1284 Weatherfield Way, San Jose, CA 95118.

German Shorthaired Pointer Club of Southern California,
Margaret Lash, HCR-3, Kettering, Lancaster, CA 93560.

High Sierra German Shorthaired Pointer Club,
Ellen Gentry, 2150 American Canyon Rd., Vallego, CA 94590.

San Joaquin German Shorthaired Pointer Club,
Estelle Lester, 7515 Vera Ave., Bakersfield, CA 93307.

German Shorthaired Pointer Club of Colorado,
Geraldine Irwin, 1101 W. Quincy, Englewood, CO 80110.

Northern Colorado German Shorthaired Pointer Club,
Dave Lyons, 345 Walnut, Ft. Collins, CO 80524.

Nutmeg German Shorthaired Pointer Club,
Eva Gorbants, 147, Old Willimantic Rd., Columera, CT 06237.

Diamond State German Shorthaired Pointer Club,
Anton Bohnt, 1004, Marl Pit Rd., Middletown, DE 19709.

German Shorthaired Pointer Club of North Florida,
Margaret Seybert, 1983 Ranchland Trail, Longwood, FL 32750.

German Shorthaired Pointer Club of Atlanta,
Cheryl Brent, 1363 Reece Rd., Woodstock, GA 30188.

German Shorthaired Pointer Club of East Idaho,
J.McCue Jnr., 190 N.Morningside Dr., Idaho Falls, ID 83402.

German Shorthaired Pointer Club of Idaho,
Mike Okamura, 11902 Alfred, Boise, ID 93704.

German Shorthaired Pointer Club of Magic Valley,
Tom Davis, RT, 1 Sunset Lane, Kimberley ID 83341.

Fort Dearborn German Shorthaired Pointer Club,
Lorraine Minkus, 666 Wrighwood, Chicago, IL 60614.

German Shorthaired Pointer Club of Illinois,
Sandy Ellinger, 1150 Parker Ave., Downers Grove, IL 60516.

German Shorthaired Pointer Club of Indiana,
Charlene Ruttar, 15405 211th St., Noblesville, IN 46060.

German Shorthaired Pointer Club of Central Iowa,
Jerry Flynn, RR 4 Winterset, IA 50237.

German Shorthaired Pointer Club of Eastern Iowa,
Julie Kessen, Box 88, Urbana, IA 52345.

North Iowa German Shorthaired Pointer Club,
Robert Nicks, 1235 North 11th St., Fort Doge, IA 50501.

Quad City German Shorthaired Pointer Club,
Garry Bussard, 2416 83rd Ave., Milan, IA 61264.

Heart of America German Shorthaired Pointer Club,
George Grubber, 1118 N.Cooper, Olathe, KS 66061.

Sunflower German Shorthaired Pointer Club,
Randy Neises, 147 S. Clarence, Wichita, KS 67213.

German Shorthaired Pointer Club of New Orleans,
Carol Florane, 1217 Zuma Ave., Metairie, LA 70003.

Mayflower German Shorthaired Pointer Club,
Linda Flynn, 189 Robbins St., Milton, MA 02186.

German Shorthaired Pointer Club of Michigan,
Matt Blades, 3344 E.Cook Rd., Grand Blanc, MI 48439.

Lansing German Shorthaired Pointer Club,
Michael Aldrich, 8324 Wiegan, Perry, MI 48872.

German Shorthaired Pointer Club of Minnesota,
Chris Sila, 313-18th Ave N., Hopkins, MN 55343.

Gateway German Shorthaired Pointer Club,
Mary Anne Delker, 1958 Duello Rd., O'Fallon, MO 63366.

German Shorthaired Pointer Club of Lincoln,
Terry Hawkins, 1330 N.79th, Lincoln, NE 68505.

German Shorthaired Pointer Club of Nebraska,
Jean Armburst, 18151 Harrison, Omaha, NE 68137.

German Shorthaired Pointer Club of Reno,
Wallace Johnson Jnr., 1170 Bounty Ct., Sparks, NV 89431.

Eastern German Shorthaired Pointer Club,
Lynn Panko, 34 Sherman St., Sewaren, NJ 07077.

German Shorthaired Pointer Club of Las Cruces,
Phyllis McNail, 1773 Webster, Las Cruces, MN 88001.

Glendale Long Island German Shorthaired Pointer Club,
Donna Vooris, 62 Mastic Blvd., Shirley, NY 11967.

Buckeye German Shorthaired Pointer Club,
Fred Ryan, 4021 McClain Rd., Lima, OH 45806.

German Shorthaired Pointer Club of Ohio,
Betsy Yates, 590 Riverside Dr., Painesville, OH 44077.

German Shorthaired Pointer Club of Oregon,
Karen Niffenegger 490 1st St., Washougal, WA 98671.

Willamette German Shorthaired Pointer Club,
Laura Wheeler, 25680 Perkins Rd., Vanenta, OR 97487.

German Shorthaired Pointer Club of Greater Pittsburgh,
Gesele Dreslinski, 4657 Gangwish St., Pittsburgh, PA 15224.

Mason Dixon German Shorthaired Pointer Club,
Marybeth Kirkland, 130 Gallop La., Maidens, VA 23102.

Schuylkill Valley German Shorthaired Pointer Club,
Judy Dietrich, 190 Gelsinger Rd., Sinking Spring, PA 19608.

Ringneck German Shorthaired Pointer Club,
Ronald Dahlman, 2416 Carmel Ct., South Sioux City, NE 68776.

El Paso del Norte German Shorthaired Pointer Club,
Jack Marczeski, 8916 Gallic Ct., El Paso, TX 79925.

German Shorthaired Pointer Club of San Antonio,
Barbara Rathmell, 14322 Farmwood, San Antonio, TX 78217.

Gulf Coast German Shorthaired Pointer Club,
Sonya Appel, 1007 Nelda, Houston, TX 77088.

Lone Star German Shorthaired Pointer Club,
Joan McGrath, 412 Sunflower La., Red Oak, TX 75154.

German Shorthaired Pointer Club of Utah,
Mark Roan, 8937 Buckingham Ct., Sandy, UT 84107.

German Shorthaired Pointer Club of Washington,
Karyn Kline, 31200 Sunrise Bch Dr., N E, Kingston, WA 98346.

Inland Empire German Shorthaired Pointer Club,
Florence Mayer, 1103 S.Christensen Rd., Medical Lake, WA 99022.

Tri-Cities German Shorthaired Pointer Club,
Clay Brown, 181 McDowell La., Selah, WA 98942.

Four Lakes German Shorthaired Pointer Club,
Frank Delmont, W 8938 Marsh Rd., Ft. Atkinson, WI 53538.

Fox Valley German Shorthaired Pointer Club,
Gerald Anderson, 1356 Lexington Ct., Oneida, WI 54155.

German Shorthaired Pointer Club of Wisconsin,
Susan Clemons, 1031, Amy Belle Rd., Germantown, WI 53022.

Southeastern Wisconsin German Shorthaired Pointer Club,
Dave Younk, 5209 Kinzie Ave., Racine WI 53406.

Woodland German Shorthaired Pointer Club,
D.Camps, 3954 Boone SW, Wyoming, MI 49509.

GERMANY
Deutsch-Kurzhaar-Verband eV, Claus Kiefer, Germersheimer Str 148, 6725 Romerberg- Berghausen (the parent club, to which are affiliated some 25 area clubs).

AUSTRIA
Osterreichischer Kurzhaar Klub,
MF Anton Hess, 3383 Inning 2.

DENMARK
German Shorthaired Pointer Club,
Henning Kromann, Hedegardsvej 8, 7323 Give.

SWEDEN
The Swedish Vorsten Club (SVC)
c/0 The Swedish Kennel Club,
5-16385 Spanga,
Sweden

FRANCE
Club Francais Du Braque Allemand,
Jean-Claude Brenard, 25 Rue Etienne Dolet, 75020 Paris.

NETHERLANDS
Nederlandse Vereniging de Duitse Staande,
C P van der Wolf, Rozeboom 11, 1541 RH Koog aan de Zaan.

NEW ZEALAND
Auckland and Regions German Shorthaired Pointer Club,
L. Allen, 8 Puketaha Rd., Henderson, Auckland.

The Continental Gundog Club,
Elsa Pymm, 6 Romesdale Rd., Papakowahai, Wellington.

Canterbury and Districts German Shorthaired Pointer Club,
Wendy Schwalger, 26 St. Johns St., Christchurch.

Otago and Southland German Shorthaired Pointer Club.

AUSTRALIA
German Shorthaired Pointer Society of New South Wales.
Carey Byrne, P.O. Box 25, Luddenham, NSW 2750.

German Shorthaired Pointer Club of Victoria.
Pat Farnan, Brenilly, 12 Glenview Rd., Launching Place, Vic.3139.

German Shorthaired Pointer Club of West Australia,
Wendy Bond, 29 Padbury Ave., Millendon, 6056 W.Australia.

German Shorthaired Pointer Club of Queensland.
Olga Gillies, Lot 4, Sunnyside La., Willowvale, Qld.4209.